RidE

jeff graft

RidE

a continental crossing
in search of trout,
clear water...and self

Crofton Creek Press
South Boardman, Michigan

This edition of *Ride: A Continental Crossing in Search of Trout, Clear Water...and Self* was printed by Jostens Book Manufacturing, State College, Pennsylvania. The book was designed by Angela Saxon of Saxon Design, Traverse City, Michigan. It is set in Cochin and printed on archival paper.

©2000 by Jeff Graft

First Edition
10 9 8 7 6 5 4 3 2 1

Published by Crofton Creek Press
2303 Gregg Road SW, South Boardman, MI 49680
www.croftoncreek.com

Printed in the United States of America

Library of Congress Cataloging-in-Publication Data

Graft, Jeff, 1967-
    Ride : a continental crossing in search of trout, clear water --and self / Jeff Graft.-- 1st ed.
        p. cm.
    ISBN 0-9700917-0-2 (alk. paper)
    1. Trout fishing--United States--Anecdotes. 2. Fly fishing--United States--Anecdotes. 3. Cycling--United States--Anecdotes. 4. Fund raising--United States--Anecdotes. 5. Graft, Jeff, 1967---Journeys--United States. I. Title.
    SH688.U6 G73 2000
    799.1'757'0973--dc21
                                            00-009304

introduction

I sat with my feet dangling over the clear water, feeling the same strange, empty feeling I always did in late summer. The summer sun was losing its punch, the days were growing mysteriously shorter, the cold iron bridge on which I sat was sucking the heat slowly from my legs, and my favorite beat-up red-and-black flannel shirt was providing just enough insulation to keep me on the verge of a shiver.

I had just fly fished my favorite stretch of river — my personal end-of-summer ritual. Tomorrow I would return to college. My mind wandered to wonderful midnight skinny dips (with the moon so bright and the water so clear you could gaze down in shoulder-deep water and still see your toes), eerie nighttime kayak rides down the Boardman River, carefree float-tube fly fishing trips on the Manistee, bluegill contests using poppers on local ponds with my buddies, and wacky explorations through swamps in search of the next magic section of river. These joys would all-too-soon turn to brutal three-a-day football workouts, four-hour chemistry labs, and long disciplined hours of physics problems in the deep, dark stacks of the library.

As I stared at my sandals and the river grunge that lingered between my toes, I realized again what an essential role northwest Michigan's rivers had played in my life. Its rivers always left me peaceful. A four-hour fly fishing session inevitably transformed my breathing to a slow and steady pace and my frenetic demeanor into a state of calm.

Early in my life, hours on the river simply translated into hours that a mischievous boy was not finding trouble. But later, the rivers took on the roles of teacher, therapist, brother, and best friend. Even later, as a businessman, the rivers came to represent valuable economic assets whose health is essential to the tourist-driven economy of the area of northern Michigan where I live.

I viewed moments spent paddling down their waters in a kayak or delicately presenting flies to their swimming inhabitants as gifts—gifts that I didn't take for granted. It would be completely self-indulgent and soulless to enjoy these gifts, as I had been so fortunate to do, and not give anything back. It was on this bridge in 1987 that I vowed to return something to the streams that had brought me so much peace, enjoyment, and growth.

Twelve years later I found myself on the same small iron bridge in late summer. But this time it was the evening before I was to leave for Washington State to start a solo bike ride across the United States. I had been fortunate to meet a group of talented and motivated professionals at the Conservation Resource Alliance (CRA) in Traverse City, Michigan. I felt a natural affinity for this lean, effective, nonprofit organization and its common-sense approach to maintaining the natural beauty and ecosystems of northern Michigan while simultaneously nurturing the economic vitality of our region.

CRA demonstrated to me that conservation efforts do not have to be built on increased regulations, lawsuits, and negative energy, but instead can flow from a greater understanding of the consequences of our interaction with our environment, the realization of the greatest economic value of our natural resources, and

The 4,000 mile cross-country route from Seattle, Washington to Savannah, Georgia.

a focus on thoughtful win-win efforts that bring people together rather than divide them.

I felt a true connection to this dedicated crew because they consistently, scientifically, and cooperatively make positive changes to the rivers of northwest Michigan. Through my bike ride, I hoped to raise awareness and funds for CRA's River Care Program, an effort designed to ensure the long-term protection of the rivers, lakes, and streams in northwest Michigan. Specifically, CRA has inventoried over ten of northern Michigan's premier watersheds and has identified approximately 2,400 problem sites—eroding banks, access sites, road crossings, and similar areas that are strangling the life from these delicate systems. Just one "average" site delivers approximately seventy tons of sediment to our streams each year. The accumulated effect of these sites can permanently destroy fisheries and wildlife habitat and degrade recreational and property values. To date, CRA and its partners have repaired 400 of these problem sites, and I was fired up to contribute to the momentum.

In the past twelve years I had found plenty of excuses to not become involved on a grass-roots level. And in each of these twelve years I performed my annual, obligatory, minimal-effort, guilt-reducing ritual of writing thirty-dollar contributions to Sierra Club, American Rivers, and the Nature Conservancy. With each year I let slip away—and with each stretch of river that now contained less healthy gravel and more ugly sediment—an uneasy, turbulent energy bubbled up within me. I resolved that to release that energy I'd do something more than simply write the annual membership. I resolved to make a cross-country bicycle ride that would raise funds for the River Care Program.

There was one minor hitch. Though I never told the fine people at CRA (they never really asked), before this ride I hadn't really cycled at all. My longest ride had been a twenty-five-miler, part of a biathlon I entered spontaneously in 1997. I intended to train intensely three months prior to the ride, but an ugly workload and travel schedule made it difficult. CRA printed 15,000 brochures promoting this event before I had even taken a training ride. I trained, briefly, on an old mountain bike that was too small for me—doing repeats up a 200-foot hill near my home. Most of those sessions occurred in the dark after 10 P.M. I managed only one training ride of any distance, fifty miles, a month or so before I left. I did not actually acquire a touring bike until a week before I departed. Did I mention I am severely handicapped when it comes to things mechanical and had never changed a bike tire before hastily doing so in my driveway that final evening?

And so I sat on my favorite bridge above my favorite river listening to the gurgle of its waters with an odd mixture of excitement, anticipation, bottled-up

frustration, and unjustified calm. The following journal was scribbled in a small spiral notebook each
evening of the ride by a tired, trout-crazed, and often
chilled wannabe cyclist who was lucky enough to see
the country, its people and its resources...and his own
life...in an entirely new way.

Here we go, let's ride.

Time to Ride

[September 12]

It is a relief to begin this ride. Before my departure, I attempted to ram seven weeks of work into three weeks. My head was still swirling when I arrived at the airport in Traverse City, Michigan, to fly to the West Coast and begin the ride. The motley crew that gathered to send me off included: My mother, who was wholeheartedly convinced that I was soon to be lambasted by a Mack truck and recommended I stay home. My father, who was slowly and reluctantly admitting to himself that perhaps I lacked the soundest decision-making skills and recommended that I more adequately think this one through. My former-Marine twin brother, who was passionate in his belief that at some point in my ride I was destined to encounter a deranged serial killer and recommended that I purchase a large, powerful handgun and head to the shooting range. My girlfriend, who felt I was certain to meet a spunky twenty-two-year-old female cyclist in Colorado and recommended that I slip into some type of male chastity device immediately.

the path is whatever passes—no end in itself.

the end is, grace—ease—

healing, not saving.

Gary Snyder from the poem "Without" in *Turtle Island*

1

In the past few months I had worked with the Conservation Resource Alliance to stimulate media interest in our event and attract national sponsors to help support the River Care cause, so the last three weeks were also filled with radio shows and TV spots. It wasn't a pleasant task, especially since I was being patted on the head for something I'd yet to accomplish. To make matters worse, I hadn't cycled much in the past, hadn't trained properly, and hadn't picked the flattest cross-country route, but one that would take me along backroads, and more important, keep me in the proximity of great trout rivers.

I chuckled as I emptied my shipping box in Everett, Washington, and sorted through the ninety disassembled pieces that would eventually become my bike. One person obviously sensed that I wasn't a cycling guru; Eric from Ralston's Bike Shop in Traverse City had included two pages of meticulous handwritten instructions on how to put this beast back together. What a warm, fluffy security blanket for an idiot two thousand miles from home. I was starting to get fired up.

The traditionally cloudy, rainy Washington coast had provided me with not just a sunny day, but a sparkling, clear, not-a-cloud-in-the-sky day. It was time to slide out of Everett and find the Pacific Ocean. I grabbed my compass, determined north, and for the only time on this trip (at least intentionally), I headed west. I pushed off and rode my first few awkward yards with the heavy panniers over both my front and rear wheels. Within a mile I noticed the front pack slipping and quickly rigged a piece of cord to attach it more adequately to the rack before I headed down the steep 500-foot hill that lay ahead. As I pulled over in a parking lot for this quick fix, an old, creaky man swaggered over to me and asked what exactly I was up to. He was more impressed that I pronounced his home state of Wisconsin properly (*Wizgonsin*, not *Wesconsin*) than he was in my bike-riding game plan.

But my mispronunciation of the town of Shewano, Wisconsin, shortly afterward had us both laughing.

I wove downhill for a few miles until I caught my first glimpse of the Pacific. Outstanding. I stopped at a grassy park with a panoramic view of Possession Sound and kicked back, lost in the view. I observed a college-aged guy and his father walking along the bluff, sucking in the great scenery. We chatted for a half-hour, the father exuding a peaceful, happy pride in his son's choice to live in the Seattle area after college graduation. I was happy that the sun shone so brightly on this show-and-tell day for the college kid, and on this sappy, ceremonious day for me.

At Possession Sound without a cloud in the sky, without proper training, without a worry, without a clue.

I saw a sign for Mukilteo State Park and decided that would be my starting point. As I headed down the final steep hill toward the park, I noticed a fun-loving group of rowdies indulging in late-morning Bloody Mary's on a restaurant deck that overlooked the Sound. With some remorse I continued, grateful that I was thirty-two years old rather than twenty-two and that tomorrow would start with a clear mind rather than a hangover.

I relaxed at a picnic table on the beach, feeling like a lucky man. Stuffing cereal into my mouth, I watched as an old dude surf cast into the gently rolling one-foot swells and two young girls played on the nearby pier. Eventually I meandered over to the perfect American family lounging in low-rider beach chairs, gazing at the scenery, and every once in a while checking out

Heading inland from the Pacific, crossing the Cascades.

the dork in the cycling shorts with the cheesy grin on his face. I talked awhile with Iener and his wife Julie. After a bit of conversation, Iener concluded that my single status was an essential parameter in this trip and that every married dude is dying for this kind of travel extravaganza. I looked at him, his kids, his beautiful wife, their cold Labatt's Blues, the lounge chairs, and the Olympic Mountains in the background and said, "Looks like you ain't got it so bad yourself."

I threw my overloaded bike on my shoulder, carried it through the soft sand to the ocean's edge, and ceremoniously dipped the rear tire into the Pacific. The moment felt nostalgic even as it was happening. I then promised myself that I was going to ride every friggin' inch of this trip, even if I had to pedal the bike through snow over the Rockies. I picked up a small red rock along the shoreline and placed it in my handlebar bag, to serve as a reminder of my starting point and my promise.

I blasted up the first 500-foot hill and then recalled that I should have set my cheap, handheld altimeter to zero while I was on the beach. Just for the exercise, I screamed back down the hill to calibrate my instrument at sea level. I rambled back uphill, pedaled about seven miles, located the Snohomish River, and began the long trek east.

As I rode I briefed myself on some self-imposed rules for this journey: (1) Bike every inch to the Atlantic, (2) Take backroads whenever possible in order to see a truer picture of America, and (3) Try not to become embedded in the grill of any semi trucks. My first backroad, Lowell Bridge Road, was closed, but I weaseled around the iron gate and chugged along a half-mile stretch of dusty, bumpy gravel road. My shiny, well-lubricated, thin-wheeled road bike was already beginning to hate my guts. But my strategy paid off; I had the next eight paved miles along the beautiful Snohomish void of any cars...and any worries.

I coasted through the quaint, historic town of Snohomish and proceeded along Highway 2 until I reached Ben Howard Drive, an awesome country road along the Skykomish River. Pedaling was not work when I had clear view of its beautiful, clear-blue water and sweet grade-two rapids. I came across a cool tree fort, barely visible in the heavy canopy of the roadside trees. My mind wandered to childhood times of exploring the woods and old forts in the acres behind our home, acres that are now subdivisions with $500,000 homes.

As I approached an expansive green field enclosed by a rough wooden fence, I noticed a gangly foal and elegant mare lackadaisically munching grass. As I pulled up to the fence to take a quick snapshot, the young horse, like an excited puppy, pranced, jumped, trotted in a large semicircle, and made a beeline for a young woman who was high stepping through the tall grass from the farmhouse a quarter mile away. The woman called, "Hey, darlin'," nuzzled her special buddy, and made her way to the old fence as both horses strung along. I enjoyed a pleasant conversation with Michelle, learning what a special bond she shared with the foal. Apparently the foal's first five days were a bit precarious, so Michelle slept in the barn with it for medical and moral support. Cool lady. She eyed my large, gear-filled panniers and my bulging tires and asked if I intended on pedaling over Stevens Pass. "One way or another," I answered.

Michelle with her "baby."

Skykomish River

I headed back on Highway 2 and received my first taste of climbing as I chugged up a few rocky hills overlooking the gorgeous Skykomish River. At dusk, I camped at the confluence of tiny Anderson Creek after a half-day's work of fifty-eight miles. I was a pretty entertaining sight as I threw my fully loaded bike over my shoulder and negotiated the steep bank, big boulders, and slippery rocks of the fast-flowing creek in my sissy cycling shoes. Setting up camp was not much of a chore, since months before I (with expert consultation from my fly fishing freak of a brother, Brad) decided to forego a tent in return for extra room in my panniers for a fly rod, pair of packable waders, and lightweight wading shoes.

I relaxed for a few minutes, reflecting on an ideal first day and deciding the only logical way to end it was to hook a few trout. The usual antsy, excited sensation that precedes all fly fishing outings overcame me as I threaded my 4-weight fly line through the delicate Orvis four-piece rod. God it was good to be alive.

I waded up to a small riffle and my heart jumped as the strike indicator twitched slightly. Within minutes I was truly were I wanted to be: gently removing a size 18 Prince Nymph from the mouth of a feisty rainbow trout, listening to the powerful sounds of rushing water, and just starting a bike ride to benefit a great conservation group. I slept soundly on a bed of baseball-sized river rock, staring at the stars before I dozed off.

LESSON: A four-piece fly rod is a much more valuable, endearing, and entertaining traveling companion than a breeze-killing, star-blocking tent.

Day 2

Over the Cascades
[September 13]

When I arrived last night the light was nearly gone from the sky, but I awoke to find this beautiful stretch of the Skykomish surrounded by the spectacular scenery of the Cascade Mountains.

I quickly ditched my bike under some brush, threw some peanut butter on a flour tortilla, grabbed my already-rigged fly rod, and headed upstream. I immediately hooked another rainbow using my Prince Nymph setup but soon switched to my true passion—dry flies. I came up empty using a couple of attractor patterns and then a Humpy, but I felt so content being in the river that I wasn't too concerned. My girlfriend, Julia, always makes fun of fly fishermen, noting that our male, results-driven, goal-oriented nature forces us to make casts for hours in order to hook fish, when in reality all we really want is to wade around in rivers and enjoy the natural beauty. I think she's probably correct. A few hours passed quickly and I suddenly remembered that perhaps I should be biking.

I pedaled along idle Highway 2, eventually finding a cozy backroad near Money Creek Campground. From the first bridge I crossed, I spotted three steelhead holding effortlessly behind boulders in deep water. Reluctantly I pushed on without fishing for them, but I rationalized the decision with the thoughts that they probably would have splintered my light 4-weight rod and I did need to cover some ground today. I ate lunch on another bridge and watched a big rainbow feed near the head of a deep pool, taking bugs off the water's smooth surface and athletically returning to its original position.

I decided to blast over Stevens Pass today even though it was already late afternoon. It was probably not the most logical decision, given how fat my bike was and how little I'd climbed before. After a couple of hours, the elevation began changing dramatically at Deception Falls (elevation 500 feet). I took a few breaks during the ensuing eight-mile, 3,500-foot climb, partly to enjoy the scenery but mainly to rest. During my limited training rides in Michigan I did some ugly repeats up hills, but the energy output and pain in those rides were usually short-lived.

During one break at approximately the three-quarter mark, I sat on the asphalt of a pullover, finished the last drop of my water, and munched on a granola bar. Between my knees I noticed a black-and-red ant hauling a horsefly-type creature four times its size. The ant attempted to carry this creature forward for a couple of feet but had to resort to pulling it backwards, wildly rotating its little ant head and antenna to monitor obstacles. The little dude was persistent, strong, and energized. Within its wee ant brain, it had not even considered failing at the task of hauling this monster back to its ant hole. The only thing I had in common with this creature at this point was the size of its wee ant brain. What a stud. I'd better keep pedaling.

Near the top I was blessed with a cascading waterfall and was able to fill both my water bottles. The temperature was falling, but the waterfall's cool spray felt great. I cranked the last mile and a half to the deserted summit. The climb was like most arduous tasks in life — brutal and seemingly impossible if thought of as one, monstrous effort but more easily tolerated if examined in smaller bite-sized pieces. I ran across a friendly French girl in the empty parking lot of the mountaintop ski area and talked with her, gradually becoming accustomed to her thick accent and picking up what she had to say. Her boyfriend, Ron, joined us and we discussed how the key to life is working extremely hard when you *are* working in order to provide longer segments of free time to follow your true passions. During all that philosophizing the sun had nearly disappeared, so I wished my new friends all the best and headed downhill to warmer air.

Whew. At the end of the first real climb of the trip.

What a rush the descent was. I was initially a bit tentative on the downhill, attempting to get a feel for how stable the bike was at high speeds with loaded panniers. It was more stable than I was, so I let it go as fast as it wanted. After seven "Yahoos" and nine miles with absolutely no pedaling, I began scouting a spot to camp. I wanted to save some of the descent for the wonderful, warm light levels of the morning.

On the crest of
the Cascade
Range, Stevens
Pass is located on
two national
forests, the Mt.
Baker-Snoqualmie
on the west side
of the crest and
the Wenatchee
National Forest
on the east.

I was a bit chilled by the time I found a quiet two-track overlooking Nason Creek. I was even stinkier than I was cold, so I took a quick skinny dip. It was the type of frigid water that immediately forces the air out of your lungs and simultaneously robs you of a majority of your manhood, if you know what I mean. While shaking the water out of my hair, squeegying the moisture off my skin, and beginning to air dry, I weighed the costs and benefits of eating and resting versus fly fishing the shallow creek. I chose fly fishing.

I threw on a couple of thick fleece jackets and silently entered the stream. I noticed two or three riffles that were a foot or two deep and had the potential to hold fish. I rigged up a size 18 Gold-ribbed Hare's Ear with a strike indicator and quietly worked upstream into casting range. I threw the softest cast I could and stuck a nice, chubby rainbow. Twenty minutes later, at dark, I thought I heard a few subtle sips in a glassy run that flowed under a hanging willow tree. I extended my 4X tippet, tied on the smallest dry fly in my box, and floated a long, sensitive-male-of-the-'90s-type cast three feet upstream from the latest rise. I was fortunate to hook another. I stopped so that the pleasant moment would linger on my relaxing stroll downstream.

Another great day. I approved of the ratio of two-thirds of a day fishing to one-third biking, but found it hard to swallow only forty-one miles covered.

LESSON: Be like an ant.

Temptations from the River Goddess

[September 14]

I began the day with four miles of wonderful downhill coasting. Although I felt the urge to hammer out some more mileage today, the tempting Wenatchee River looked too beautiful to pass by. Ten miles into my day, I approached an empty campground and crossed a bridge spanning the river. Drool slowly rolled down my chin and landed softly into the fast moving water fifty feet below as I gawked at the beautiful, fishable riffles.

Wenatchee National Forest covers 2.1 million acres, approximately 40% of it designated as wilderness.

Nymphing appeared to be the best way to fish these fast runs, yet I only had one small split-shot left from yesterday's excursion. I scoured the vacant, rustic campground in a vain attempt to round up enough split-shot for the day. I was fortunate to find a station wagon tucked into the trees belonging to a chap named Phil. As he dug out a few miscellaneous pieces of lead for me from inside his packed vehicle, he described how he, his wife, and two-year-old had just completed a one-month cross-country camping trip. The simultaneous thought of "Man, I'd hate to be this guy" rose to both our minds as he examined my rock-hard bike seat and I witnessed the high-pitched wailing of his young son.

I fished for about four hours, the highlight coming when a large rainbow swiped my Prince Nymph, dove into a tangle of sunken tree branches, and tied a few fancy knots before escaping. Hiking back to my bike along the thick, overgrown riverside trail, I wondered where I would find the discipline to concentrate on biking when my route purposely ran along so many beautiful rivers.

Continuing on my bike, I followed the Wenatchee, spotting monster salmon lazily heading upstream. In

one large, deep bend that held at least one hundred fish, I stopped, sat sideways on my bike seat with my feet propped up on the guardrail, and watched the big males jostle each other. I remembered landing a big salmon using my buddy Matt's 6-weight (after my 10-weight had exploded on a large fish the day before) a few

Lingering at a stream crossing to look for trout.

years ago in Michigan and began calculating how aggressive (ignorant) I wanted to get with my tiny 4-weight.

My daydream was interrupted by Phil, who had passed me in his jam-packed station wagon, performed a heroic U-turn, and was now excitedly walking towards me. "Hey," he said, "I learned this whole section of river, including the one you just fished, is closed—and the place is crawling with rangers." I am the conservation-minded, catch-and-release, barbless-hook fisherman, but obviously not the intelligent and well-researched type. Time to pedal.

An hour later on another crossing of the Wenatchee, I watched as fearless teenage boys screamed with delight as they leapt off the bridge into the clear water below. At the end of the bridge I talked awhile with a peaceful looking dude with John Denver glasses and his scruffy looking buddy. After a pleasant conversation, the dirty looking fellow commented, "You may have just crossed Stevens Pass, but you still don't know what mountains are about. Colorado has real mountains, and you're a fool for trying to scale them in late fall." I am not certain of the exact challenge that lies ahead, though I am certain that weasel's words will provide a little extra incentive.

Crossed another bridge over the Wenatchee and watched fourteen-inch rainbows lying behind the salmon and eating the salmon eggs. Took a granny-gear tour of Leavenworth—clean, Bavarian-style town—and then pedaled hard until I got east of Cashmere and slid off the highway onto Sleepy Hollow Road, a fantastic, easy-going route that followed the Wenatchee River. Spotted salmon stacked like cordwood.

Went through the old town of Monitor, a quaint fruit-growing community. Bought a can of ravioli for dinner—right out of the can, baby. Pedaled into the twilight to just south of Lincoln Rock State Park and found an orchard of mature apple trees. Pushed the bike deep into a row of trees and nearly passed out on my tarp before I could unroll my sleeping bag and bivy sack.

LESSON: Never listen to those who tell you what you can't do.

Day 4

A Cold Shower
[September 15]

Half woke to cold, heavy dew at 5 A.M. and heard the rumble of an old pickup. Gradually a red fifties-style pickup came into focus as it made its way through the orchard. "Great," I thought, "watch this dude start squirting me with some lethal pesticide."

Then water began spraying out of sprinkler heads everywhere around me. I made a mad dash to grab my well-soaked clothes, sleeping bag, and biking shorts that were scattered about. I rolled them into a ball and tried to push my bike through the tall grass, dropping gear and frantically picking it up as I ran.

I finally gave up and let the orchard's irrigation rain down on me, laughing as I slowly pushed my bike onto the two-track out of sprinkler range. An old weathered man appeared and said in broken English, "Sorry, no see you."

Escaping the orchard, wet but unbowed.

"No problema!" I said.

I rode a frigid eight miles in forty-something-degree weather to Orondo and pulled into a small convenience store. A whole electric line crew was drinking coffee at a table. They stared at me as I walked in, probably thinking, "Look at that boy in the cute, tight, wet shorts." I talked with them for a while in my manliest tone.

Began the climb through Corbaley Canyon, which yesterday I inaccurately analyzed as a 300-foot climb...2,200 feet later I reached the top.

A flag crew, outfitted with walkie-talkies, was working along the road up, and they assured me that they had a nice cold Budweiser waiting for me at the top. The beerless, toothless flag guy at the peak smiled and laughed at me as I passed by. All in good fun.

The plateau was a cool contrast from the dry sand canyon hills—beautiful sunshine poured down on endless fields of harvested wheat. I stopped, emptied my panniers of all the wet stuff, stripped down to my bike shorts, and dried my gear in the field of harvested stubble. I kicked back, enjoyed the awesome scenery, and surveyed my thirty-yard path of littered socks, shorts, and fleece. Six cars stopped in the twenty minutes it took to dry my stuff to take a picture they will probably entitle, "Stupid, half-naked guy drying his gear with cool scenery in the background."

So far I have made a few mistakes in assuming labeled locations on my map were actually towns (like Farmer and Highland). Unfortunately, they are just intersections now, so I had a few long stretches with no water.

Made it to Coulee City and the Dry Falls Dam on the Columbia River. Even though dams are a clean source of energy, I get bummed thinking how visually beautiful the area was before man's intrusion and how much damage the dams inflict on migrating fish species and aquatic life.

In an effort to hammer out a few more miles, I pedaled until after dark. I wasn't quite sure where to throw down my sleeping bag since the whole area was rattlesnake-infested sagebrush, but then, like a beacon of light, a goal post from a football field grabbed my eye. I snaked my way onto the field, enjoying the only patch of grass in forty miles. I moved the players' bench underneath the goal posts, cooked a hearty concoction of pasta and tuna, and enjoyed a clear, wide-open sky filled with stars.

Today I traveled seventy-one miles in warm sunshine.

LESSON: Rarely is it worth getting upset at something that does not go according to plan.

Wild steelhead and Pacific salmon are in serious trouble on the Columbia and Snake rivers. Conservation groups have called for the removal of four dams on the lower Snake to restore threatened and endangered salmon and steelhead stocks.

American Rivers has labeled the Snake River the nation's most endangered river for the year 2000.

Mission: 100-Miler

[September 16]

Woke up underneath the goal post. No available fishing, no drastic climbs ahead of me today—time to hammer out a hundred-miler you sissy.

This was the fifth day in a row with cloudless weather. I started each day wearing two fleece jackets, a stocking cap, gloves, and a windbreaker, but each morning I'd be shirtless within an hour.

Found the route through Almira, Wilbur, and Davenport to be much of the same rolling sagebrush country. Seems like I climbed at least sixty 50- to 100-foot hills. My bulging, unaerodynamic panniers do not allow for much high-speed coasting on the downhills, but that's the price for bringing along Gore-Tex waders and wading boots. I'll be giggling in Idaho.

Talked with a host of farmers, retirees, and other folks at each convenience store who said they'd all be willing to pitch in and buy me a motorcycle. A beer truck driver finally approached me in Wilbur and said, "I've passed you six times today and shook my head each time." I scolded him for not tossing out a cold frosty beverage to me at least once.

A bearded chap in Davenport offered me a place to stay at around 5 P.M., but I told him I was on a mission from God to hit 100 miles today. Jeremiah ended up being the owner of a local bike shop and gave me detailed instructions on how to avoid traffic around Spokane and how to access the Centennial Bike Trail that connects Spokane to Coeur d'Alene, Idaho.

Pedaled hard the last thirty-five miles to Spokane and screamed down the hill on Sunset Boulevard. Received instructions from a skateboarder who promised me he was riding across America as soon as he got his bike fixed. Talked with a dude with what appeared to be a knitting needle rammed through his nose, and received instructions to River Front Park from a corporate logistical expert who works part of the year in Antarctica.

River Front Park was beautiful and Spokane had a nice feel as far as cities go, but I was on a mission. Finished the last eleven miles along the bike trail using my Maglite and nearly twisted my bike around the cement no-access poles that guard the trail from motorized vehicles. On one ambiguously marked section of the trail, or perhaps I was just out of it, I somehow drifted off the trail and found myself in a warehouse district. I spotted a woman at one of the loading docks and struck up a conversation with this friendly, Popeye-forearmed hulk of a lady. As I helped her lift the last two boxes into the warehouse, she described life in Spokane and gave me directions back to the path.

We sat with our feet dangling over the loading dock, and for a moment, I laid back to stretch my kinked vertebrae. Her words blurred and I was asleep within three seconds of being horizontal. I startled awake after what could only have been a five-second nap, popped up, shook her hand, and headed back into the surreal darkness.

Rode up to a quiet area near a group of colonial-style buildings and passed out underneath a monstrous willow tree, maintaining my low-cost, low-impact, stealth-camping strategy.

Good effort today—102 miles with lots of little hills and sunshine.

LESSON: Hundred-milers will only be easy if I don't gab for hours with locals at gas stations.

The Joys of a Truck-Stop Shower

[September 17]

Discovered I was on the grounds of a child foster-care complex when I awoke. In the final stages of my delirious flashlight ride last night, I had once again strayed off the Centennial Bike Trail.

I stopped at a fruit stand and grabbed a huge handful of peaches and nectarines. The jovial ladies there wouldn't let me pay for the fruit and gave me instructions in life ("You go, boy") and directions back to the trail. I followed the well-designed trail along the Spokane River. Beautiful morning.

Decided to take my first shower of the trip at a truck stop. The combination shower and bacterial petri dish was good enough for me. You know you're dirty when you need to soak in the hot shower for a few minutes before soap and shampoo even have a chance to penetrate the oily, dirty scum.

Spent half of the day on the phone doing business and ensuring that I would have a job when the ride is finished. Headed south on Route 95 out of Coeur d'Alene along the western shore of the town's beautiful lake. At a gas station, I was approached by two fish-crazed wild men trailing a huge bass boat who tempted me with a two-day fishing trip and an easy way to cover 200 miles. I resisted.

I was greeted with a relatively kind 700-foot climb out of town and nice vistas. Found that Route 95 is a two-lane road with about a six-inch paved shoulder. Ouch.

Down the length of Idaho, climbing and screaming downhill all the way.

Crashed (slept) along the road in some scrub bordered by pine trees.

LESSON: Sometimes you may be actually cleaner covered in your own filth and free of fungi, bacteria, and transmitted diseases than you are after a nice hot shower in a truck stop.

Blessed Gluttony

[September 18]

Heavy frost covered my stocking cap and bivy—entirely too cozy in my sleeping bag for the 6 A.M. wake-up call. I allowed the sun to ease over the hills in the east and to thaw and eventually dry my gear.

Felt like a casual day. Zipped down Route 95 until I reached a sparkling new gas station. I spotted two yuppie couples on motorcycles and amused them in my effort to trade my bike and gear for one of their Harleys. We enjoyed a lively conversation that coincidentally ended at about the time I opened a can of Chef Boyardee and began happily gobbling it.

Near Worely, I headed east on Conkling Park Road. It was a real pleasure to get off the narrow shoulder and away from the sound of cars. Encountered beautiful farms and rolling hills that ran into Chatcolet Lake, just south of Coeur d'Alene Lake. Fantastic view from the hillside of the calm water and evergreen-lined mountains.

Hauled down the twisting and narrow road, smoking those brakes, until I was lakeside. Hiked near Plummer Creek marsh—a wonderfully vibrant wetland filled with lush plants, the sounds of nature, and wildlife that included wood ducks, muskrats, and kingfishers.

Followed the ups and downs of Route 5 until I reached St. Maries. A guy with a roadside fruit stand saw me working hard up the last hill near St. Maries with my full panniers and said, "Come on over son, you still gots lots of room in those packs for a watermelon or two."

In St. Maries I rapped with the boys in a fly shop and then actually had a sit-down meal in a café on

Main Street. I gorged myself on chicken breast and four full trips to the salad bar. Two off-duty truck drivers cracked jokes each time I pillaged the salad cart, shaking their heads in disbelief at my aggressive grazing, though from the size of their fuel tanks it appeared they had done much of the same.

I headed out of town and came across a young couple who had just shot a bear and had it proudly displayed atop the dog kennel in the back of their pickup truck. That's not exactly my bag, but it was fun hearing their excited story of the big hunt.

Mack-trucked my way up a 700-foot climb, receiving lots of beeps and thumbs up from passing cars whose occupants undoubtedly felt sorry for the stupid guy with the overloaded bike. With my snail-like uphill pace, I was able to spot a few slightly bruised peaches on the shoulder that had fallen off a fruit truck. Of course, I grubbed them down.

The bear hunter with her prize.

St. Marie's, Idaho

The most enjoyable part of this touring sport is that it is possible to eat outrageous quantities of food and not gain weight, maybe even lose a little. Today I ate sixteen Pop-Tarts between four large meals. Life is good!

My favorite time to pedal is between 6 P.M. and 7 P.M. when the light levels have fallen, the sun has cooled, and the traffic dies.

Spotted some twenty deer along the road as I headed south toward Fernwood. At around 9 P.M. I found a small cow pasture to call home for the evening.

Since I exuded some of the same odors as the residents of the pasture, my presence was barely noticed.

Another beautiful, sunny day. Lackadaisically covered sixty-three miles.

LESSON: If you enjoy consistently eating to the point of gluttony but don't want the downside of rapid and grotesque weight gain, bike touring is your sport.

Day 8

Into Clearwater Canyon
[September 19]

Realized in the morning that I had blindly placed my sleeping bag in the only manure-free coordinate in the entire pasture. Nice work.

Hurriedly pedaled to check out the stretch on the St. Maries that the guys at the fly shop had spoken of. Eight miles later I found it to be unimpressive—low water levels, no current or cover. Perhaps they're just like those of us in northern Michigan who send the tourists to the lousy fishing spots. Hah!

South of the town of Clarkia the calm of my morning ride was interrupted by the scream of motocross bikes. I popped into Fossil Bowl, a locally famous motocross course carved out of the mountain, and watched boys aged four to forty tool around the course. It was entertaining to watch them fly over the jumps as I grubbed on French toast and eggs. I looked and smelled especially grungy today and therefore didn't attract many conversations. I can always tell when I start looking unshaven, dirty, and scraggly because convenience store attendants, little girls, and nice old ladies look my way and then quickly turn to avoid eye contact.

Followed the Potlatch River into the sleepy, unconscious town of Bovill. While grabbing an OJ and filling my water bottles at the café in town, I met three hunters having dinner. They were extremely nice, but definitely men of few words. They appeared to be highly trained masters of one-syllable sentences composed of unique grunts and grumblings. I did a quick three-minute shave in the café restroom and headed out. Followed Route 3 and enjoyed a sweet four-mile, 1,500-foot curving descent into Kendrick. Even my bloated bike hit forty miles per hour. I enjoyed the road to myself since most of the logging trucks take weekends off.

Talked for a while with some Kendrick high schoolers near the grocery store, grabbed some food, kicked my cycling shoes off, and stuffed my face in the shade of the building. A nice off-duty park ranger asked my story as I plowed through two cold cans of chunky soup and an entire package of Fig Newtons. She told me of her experiences in the Peace Corps, described conservation efforts in Idaho, and after ten minutes, bid me farewell. I checked my bloated belly for stretch marks as I mounted my trusty bike and eased back down the road. After covering ten miles, the park ranger pulled her truck in front of me and generously invited me to a dinner she was cooking for her buddies. She'd traveled enough to know how much a dirt-bag traveler appreciates a warm meal, clean clothes, and a hot shower. But it was only midafternoon and I needed to knock out some miles, so I reluctantly declined the offer after a dozen thank yous.

Followed Route 3 until it intersected the Clearwater River and Route 12. The Clearwater was beautiful and wide. But I'd told myself that I was going to hit 100 miles this day no matter what, so I cranked it hard for forty miles past Kendrick.

The Clearwater National Forest is nestled on the west side of the Bitterroot Mountains in north-central Idaho.

It was difficult to find a spot to sleep as I followed Clearwater Canyon; there was water on the left side, the canyon wall on the right. Finally at 9:30 P.M. I found a spot in Greer overlooking the river, which I watched flowing by in the light of a three-quarter moon.

Another picturesque day—300 miles covered so far. Too much talking.

Lesson: While touring, the degree to which people interact with you is inversely proportional to the amount of scraggly scruff on your face.

Heart of the Monster

[September 20]

The North Fork of the Clearwater is one of Idaho's most popular rafting and fishing rivers. The upper stretch contains several big rapids, including a boulder-choked class IV-V drop called Irish Railroad.

Ninth day of sunshine in a row. Chalk it up to good clean living. Coasted through Greer. This small, old town was still asleep. I would love to have blasted east on State Road 11 and fished the North Fork of the Clearwater, but I'm attempting to make this a two-month rather than a two-year trip.

I think this trip has reinforced that the most special places to fly fish are found at the end of brutal two-tracks and tough two-day hikes. Being confined to where a gravel-hating touring bike will take me often leads to less optimal spots.

Clearwater Canyon was a combination of the most beautiful and at the same time the most dangerous stretch I've been on yet. The shoulder is on average eight inches wide and often drops off into a ditch. Add to that the possibility of being easily distracted by rising fish in the river below and the fact that this serpentine road is heavily traveled by logging trucks, and it's easy to see why it is a unique challenge.

I found a few irresistible stretches of water in this beautiful country that needed to be fly fished. I hiked the bluffs while attempting to spot fish in the clear water below. There were dozens of large mountain whitefish hanging near the deep end of pools and small fish rising at the surface. Stubborn as I am, and confident that I can delicately present a fly to any fish no matter what species and hook it, I had to have a go at it. I got out my four-piece rod, donned waders and wading boots, and scrambled down the bank only to have these micro fish reject all six flies I tried.

Along the banks I found huge blackberries and ate them by the handful. Pretty convenient since I had no breakfast. Suddenly, seven-thirty in the morning turned into two in the afternoon, and I had no food or water and was sixteen miles from Kamiah, the nearest town. I decided it was time to put it in gear. Still, another cocky fish rose eight miles into my thirsty journey and I couldn't resist, so I did the quick change into wading gear, got in the river again, and threw the gentlest cast I could muster onto the calm, clear water. Humbled again.

I reached Kamiah a parched fishing fool. I entered the grocery store and immediately drank three-quarters of a gallon of Sunny Delight and bought groceries as though I was going to load them into a station wagon. After handling an assortment of errands, I rode leisurely south toward Kooskia.

Stopped at a sacred Nez Perce Indian spot called "Heart of the Monster." Native American legend says that "Coyote," in an effort to stop "Monster" from eating the various animals in the area, destroyed the beast and scattered his body parts throughout the Northwest. The various Indian tribes sprang up where these body parts landed. The heart, which landed right here on the Clearwater River, gave way to the Nez Perce. The fenced-off mound did appear heart-shaped. Cool stuff.

Later I read a placard of how Lewis and Clark on their return east spent six weeks at this site on the Clearwater waiting out deep snows on Lolo Pass. I crossed the bridge into Kooskia and watched a huge beaver swim upstream directly below me. Outstanding close-up view of the way he used his legs and tail for propulsion. Great moment in the fading light of day.

At twilight I passed a yard with four dogs. Like dogs a dozen times before on this trip, these put on a tough act and then had their attack thwarted by a chain link fence. As I passed them, I noticed an exceptionally eager look on their doggy faces, but seeing the fence I teased, "Nah, nah, nah...nah!" As I passed, I knew they'd run to the far edge of their yard and have to put on the brakes at the fence. Predictably, these rascals came ripping across the yard to the driveway. Problem was there was no fence there. Aaaagh! Now I had four dogs chasing me—three Australian shepherds (fast ones) and a sleek, pissed-off Doberman with ears back and teeth exposed.

All I saw in my mind as I sprinted was a Doberman mouth with sharp teeth slashing through my panniers. I am glad my legs were fresh from a sissy day of pedaling. The Doberman was the only real threat, but it gave up after two-tenths of a mile.

Pedaled until dark. Found a sweet cow pasture right on the South Fork of the Clearwater. The ground may not have been as hard as concrete, but it was definitely in the league of fresh asphalt.

LESSON: A night on hard, rocky ground with an open sky filled with stars is more restful to the soul than one on a soft bed with a mind filled with self-manufactured deadlines and pressures.

The Middle Fork of the Clearwater and the Lochsa rivers are part of the National Wild and Scenic River system.

Trout Fever, Again

[September 21]

Woke up a few times last night to deer snorting. I'm sure they were wondering what this stinky, frost-covered guy was doing in their stomping grounds.

Took a nippy ride into Harvester. Found an RV park with a convenience store and entered the store under the stare of seven old cronies seated at a table. It brought back the words of the Bob Seger tune, "...and you feel the eyes upon you, as you're shakin' off the cold. You pretend it doesn't bother you, but you just want to explode..."

They just must not see many men wander into the store in biking shorts on thirty-degree mornings. As I made my way past their table, clippety-clipping across the wooden floor in my cycling shoes, I watched them, watching me, watching them.

Warmed up quickly as I climbed 2,000 feet in four to five miles and entered the town of Grangeville. With no breakfast, I was hurting, so I did one of those eat-eggs-and-pancakes-till-you-virtually-puke things at a cool little restaurant. Stopped across the street at a sports store attempting to halfway settle my bloated stomach and met a good-spirited boxer dog that was guarding the place with a happy wagging tail.

Climbed another 900 feet as I left Grangeville and received a few supportive honks. Finally reached about 4,100 feet eight miles north of White Bird and began screaming downhill all the way into town—a winding grade of 7 percent. Lots of yee-hahs on that one, reaching a sustained forty miles per hour with no traffic on the road.

Screeched to a halt halfway down—my brakes hate it when I do that—to check out the Nez Perce war battlefield of the Battle of White Bird Canyon. On this range over a hundred years ago, a cagey group of Nez Perce warriors took out one-third of a cavalry unit. The Nez Perce did not lose a single man that day. It was eerie to look on the battlefield below and imagine the flesh-and-blood struggle that was so cooly depicted on the historic site's diagram.

I finished the descent into the small, aged town of White Bird. Entered a small café and thought I was going to be humming that Bob Seger tune again, but I actually ended up talking with the waitress and very nice couple originally from Colorado. They had a radio scanner and received a report that a murderer just escaped from the correctional facility in Grangeville and had just told his priest that he wanted to go down in a blaze of glory. Nice. I guess the locals call the facility the "Catch-and-Release" because of its escape record.

Site of the Nez Perce battle near White Bird, ID.

I continued on Highway 95 and got my first glimpse of the mighty Salmon River. Awesome. I followed it, drooling for a few miles and then spotted upstream a flotilla of rafts coming my way. I stopped at a bluff close to the river and waited ten minutes for them to pass. They harassed me about how hard I was working compared to them, and a couple of the rowdies dove off the rafts into the cool water just to rub it in.

I hauled a couple more miles and found a well-groomed park on the river and took a wonderful swim. A real contrast to the 2,900-foot climb in eighty-degree weather. A park ranger showed me where to pick grapes and figs in the nearby scrub. Stopped at a local fruit stand and inhaled a couple of juicy peaches.

As I biked the bluff along the river I noticed a trout or two rising, and then came across a stretch in which I spotted four rises in thirty seconds. I leaned my bike along the guardrail, grabbed my fly fishing gear, and rumbled down the steep rocky bank. Instead of using waders I just kicked off my cycling shoes and bumbled and stumbled across the Crisco-covered rocks until I reached a nice centrally located flat one.

I could tell they were cutthroats feeding on small gnats and knew I had nothing in my box small enough to match the hatch.

From the road I heard a yell and spotted a fellow cyclist loaded down much like me. His name was Ryan, it turned out, and he also was attempting a cross-country bike trip. As we screamed to each other over the flow of the river, I learned that he had begun his journey in Virginia and therefore was much closer to finishing his ride than I was. Half of me wanted to scurry up the rocky hill, give this dude a high-five, compare gear, swap stories, and exchange philosophies. But my addiction to trout fishing left me virtually paralyzed. We were temporarily heading in the same direction, but the possibility of my smallest-sized Adams hooking a cutthroat was an even stronger lure than riding with a companion for a while. Trout fever strikes, again.

It turned into an awesome evening as the light level fell and a deer edged its way to the river for a drink. I rode another dreamy twenty miles in the dark to Riggins; a full moon and gusts of warm air funneling through the canyon made it a sweet ride. Certain moments in life seem to stick in your mind, perhaps forever. That ride, with the moon glistening off the Salmon River and casting a shadow of the eastern mountains

After gold was discovered in Nez Perce territory in 1860, the tribe was forced to surrender all of its lands and return to a reservation at Lapwai. A band led by Chief Joseph refused to accept the agreement, leading to the battle with federal troops near White Bird. Following the battle, the band began a desperate retreat of over 1,100 miles, pursued all the way by a much larger force of federal troops. About 30 miles from the Canadian border, Joseph and his band were captured and sent to Oklahoma where many died. Today the Nez Perce National Historic Trail marks the historic route.

onto the western canyon wall, will be one of them.

Instead of staying in Riggins, I scouted for a spot along the highway where I could bed down near the river. I parked my bike on the empty side of the road and walked down to the river's edge only to hear the gust from a passing truck knock my bike over. Oh well. Two cars saw my fallen bike with no rider and stopped. I rushed up, flashed my Maglite a couple of times to signal that I was okay. I crashed on a little grassy cubbyhole right near the river. Great night.

Nice day of pedaling—sixty-five miles with a 2,900-foot climb.

LESSON: The true appreciation of life comes in its contrasts—brutal climbs suddenly transformed into exhilarating downhills; thirst and hunger giving way to bloated contentment; hard work and heat dissipating quickly into the refreshing cool waters of a river.

Day 11

Kick It

[September 22]

Actually experienced a warm night in which I wasn't forced to bury my head in my stinky sleeping bag.

Pedaled a mile or two to Riggins and arrived right as Ryan, the cyclist I'd met on the river, was leaving the RV camp he had stayed at. We were able to pedal forty miles south together to New Meadows until he headed west to Portland and I traveled east toward McCall. Cool dude. I asked why he was pedaling four thousand miles. He said, "To kick it."

He had a flat tire ten miles into our journey and the repair job gave me ample time to grub down some peanut butter for breakfast and thoroughly psychoanalyze him and his relationship with his girlfriend back home. Turns out he fell in love last week with a mountain girl in Missoula during the Rocky Mountain Oyster Festival. I spent the next thirty miles giving him unrequested and contradictory advice regarding his predicament.

Ryan doing a little roadside repair.

Riggins, ID

Without really realizing it, we climbed 1,500 feet against the wind as we followed the Little Salmon River. Along the way I spotted a man and his wife rigging their fly rods near a beautiful stretch of river. I, of course, pulled off to shoot the shit with my fly fishing brother and sister while Ryan contemplated whether or not I suffered from some weird obsessive-compulsive disorder. After twenty-five minutes of fly fishing stories, I was extremely proud of myself for jumping back on my bike and not indulging in a bit of angling myself.

Ryan and I took turns drafting behind each other in the moderate wind. It seemed to cut our energy output in half. Traveling together definitely made the pedaling easier, and it didn't force me to resort to the bag of mind-game tricks I use to motivate myself during difficult stretches. We arrived in New Meadows, found a small café, kicked our shoes off, and stretched out in a large booth. As I looked over at Ryan, it seemed as though I'd known him for years, even though it had only been a matter of hours. The bond of common toil and a common mission deepened our short time together. We ate like horses, headed out to our bikes, tweaked our panniers, shook hands, looked each other in the eye, and sincerely wished each other the best.

Solo once again, I pumped up a steep 7-percent, 1,200-foot climb to McCall. Beautiful country. Enjoyed the two-mile coast into town and the great view of Payette Lake. Shared life stories for forty minutes with a couple clerks at an outdoor store, unaware that I kept them well past closing time. Genuinely friendly people in McCall.

That night I camped along a picturesque stretch of the North Fork of the Payette River. I did a casual wade upstream at twilight, but water levels were low and I found no deeper pools that might hold fish in the shingle water that I waded. Spent a peaceful night on a grassy bluff overlooking an expansive bend of the river.

Climbed 3,700 feet and covered fifty-three miles. My jaw is a bit sorer than my legs today.

Lesson: Synergies definitely exist between humans that allow their combined energies to be greater than the sum of their individual efforts.

Day 12

Roadkill

[September 23]

Heavy mist coming off the river below as I crawled out of the sleeping bag. Headed south using backroads to stay off Highway 55. Enjoyed a peaceful drive down

Farm to Market Road. Cool name, cool road. Wide-open fields, mountains in the background, and quaint old houses and churches gave the road and the "town" of Roseberry a homey feel.

Eventually I had to cycle on Highway 55 and found it bicycle friendly. Enjoyed an unheard-of twenty miles of relatively flat ground in which I was able to average seventeen miles per hour, but I was slapped back to reality with a quick 400-foot climb just north of Cascade.

Performed my now routine act of heading to the grocery store, gulping a half gallon of OJ as I picked the rest of my morsels from the aisles, heading to the shady side of the building, plopping down next to my bike with my cycling shoes off, and talking with the locals as they entered and left the store.

Of course, when they first approach me and my circle of grub, I snarl and growl big like a dog does when you get too close to its chow bowl. Talked with a very nice lady and her two boys who were originally from Colorado and have relatives from Salida, Colorado, which will be the site of my buddy Matty Brown's Pig Roast and Fly Fishing Extravaganza on October 7 to be attended by the most pathetic, trout-crazed, beer-dependent river dogs I know, including this one if the road gods are kind. I invited her also.

Ran into a macho headwind out of town that burned up approximately six of the eight Pop-Tarts I had for dessert. A bridge was out north of Smiths Ferry and traffic was backed up a bit as the four guys who were working and the twenty-two who were watching did their thing.

Talked with a man in Smiths Ferry who said that I had been blessed with exceptionally mild weather so far. He said that in some years they've had two feet of snow here by October 15—so get moving, boy! Yes, but it's only September 23 and I have a bit of fly fishing to do.

I enjoyed a wonderful treat as I left Smiths Ferry—some twenty continuous miles of downhill. The perfect kind of downhill. I coasted at about eighteen miles per hour—not too fast, not too slowly—with only the occasional need to pedal. As I was enjoying this free ride, I was able to follow the beautiful North Fork of the Payette River, giving the "pump it up" sign to whitewater kayakers I passed. Rode along some angry white water, close up. Gazed at the mountains and sucked in the smell of evergreens. I loved moments such as this one—no need to cognitively determine whether you are filled with joy, you simply observe and feel.

My dream world ended when I was forced to leave the downhill route that still stretched before me to the south and take another uphill route that would lead me east to Lowman. This was a critical turn-off—one that rejected the faster, simpler, easier route to Boise and then over to Pocatello—and accepted the scenic, mountainous, climb-filled route that included Stanley, Ketchum, and the Sawtooth Mountains. My legs will hate my guts.

I followed the clear South Fork of the Payette River and five miles into my turn-off I spotted three dark monster trout all rise for the same bug at the same time. Moments later, I saw two big brown-colored fish gracefully porpoise at the surface and dive down into a deep pool. My heart pumped until I realized it was a group of four otters working a clear pool. It was great watching them gracefully dive and surface as a team.

It took me some ten minutes to sneak down the rocky bank to within twenty feet of them. I timed my movement to coincide with their dives. I watched close up for four to five minutes until one of the boys saw me and began snorting to the others. They all startled as they saw me and swam upstream and snorted, downstream and snorted, and then returned to the same pool, snorting.

Down the road a bit I came across a huge deer

carcass. Its whole body was in motion as thousands of maggots worked their decomposition magic on him. There lay death and life.

I skated down a lonely two-track and ended up right at the river. Unbelievably beautiful. It was close to dark, so I quickly grabbed my waders and rigged my fly rod with a Woolly Bugger. I stayed relatively close to shore as I waded because the ultra-clear water and low-light conditions made rocks that were five feet deep appear to be in six inches of water. It was great feeling the fat thirteen-inch rainbow smack my Woolly Bugger. The end of a great day.

Covered seventy-seven miles without working especially hard.

LESSON: Ride hard, laugh lots, suck the juice out of life. Whether you believe in an after-life or not, we're all going to end up in the exact same state as that deer on the side of the road.

Day 13

Magical Rivers, Bulldog Fish

[September 24]

Woke up in the middle of a dream about my old Alma College football team, so I was all pumped up and ready to fly fish. Had the pleasure of greeting the day watching a chubby thirteen-inch rainbow slowly rise from behind a boulder in a four-foot run and gently suck in my grasshopper pattern.

The only thing gentle about these fish was the way they slowly and efficiently rose to grab a fly. The rest of my interaction with them was combative. These rainbows and cutthroats brawled and battled to the very end—even squirming and shaking as I attempted to release them.

I fished without breakfast and arrived ravenous at my campsite in the late afternoon. I was virtually out of food—only a scrape or two left in my peanut butter jar.

I meticulously scraped the last ounce onto my flour tortilla, set it on my bike seat, tossed the plastic jar in my garbage sack, and watched in slow motion as a gust of wind gently lifted my tortilla off the saddle and tipped it face down into the pine needles and dirt below. Considering a submission of my Extra Natural Crunchy recipe to Skippy.

Biked to Garden Valley to run errands in the late afternoon and then gazed at the scenery as I covered a mere fifteen miles. Spread my tarp over bumpy ground directly overlooking a calm stretch of the South Fork of the Payette. Got lost watching the river roll by. There is always magic when we're close to water— perhaps it ties us to our origins in the womb. But a static lake doesn't have the same appeal as moving, dynamic, sound-producing rivers. Rivers are able to touch every sense.

LESSON: Don't give up, especially during points of the battle in which everyone expects you to.

The Sting of Autumn

[September 25]

With a little cloud cover last night, the sleeping was actually a bit balmy, making it that much easier to get back on the bike saddle in the morning.

This is by far the most beautiful stretch I've hit thus far. Followed the Ponderosa Pine Scenic Byway to Lowman, then another sixty miles to Stanley.

It truly felt like fall today—warm golds, browns, and reds in the brush near the South Fork, crisp air that allows you to see forever, and gusts of wind that produce those traditional autumn sounds of dry leaves blowing across the fields and road.

Encountered another downhill safety hazard—sharp ponderosa pine needles being whipped off the trees by the strong gusts of wind and striking my arms and face like darts.

Had a nice heart-to-heart with a man working in a small grocery store in Lowman about what it means to him to live a satisfied, isolated existence out in the mountains of Idaho. His main point was that you only have perhaps two true friends at a time in life and he has them here. Here in Lowman he avoids most of the niceties and social posturing associated with living in more populated areas.

Depending on how hard the autumn wind blew and the severity of climb, I alternated about eighty times between going shirtless and wearing a fleece jacket with a windbreaker. Had a memorable 35-mph downhill ride that was slowed quickly by a forceful uphill wind. It was a strange sensation to have to pedal a steep downhill—and even stranger to be moving only 10 mph when I did pedal.

A view of the Sawtooth Mountains, just outside of Stanley, Idaho.

Climbed 4,000 feet and covered seventy-seven miles today—not that painful. The beauty of the mountains and the motion of the South Fork and Canyon Creek sucked most of the burn out of my legs.

Stopped in Stanley to spend the night. The wind was gusting so I picked a spot in a field behind a three-foot mound of dirt. Spent one of the coldest nights of my life in a medium-weight sleeping bag under the stars. It was one of those sleeps in which you expend so much energy shivering and attempting to stay warm that in the morning you feel like you've run a marathon.

LESSON: Even in the complex, high-tech world we live in, true tests in life that foster growth often are ones that are extremely ground level and basic—lack of food, water, warmth, death of loved one…

Day 15

Trout Gods Beckon
[September 26]

My two water bottles were frozen solid in the morning. Unfortunately, I had forgotten to put them in my sleeping bag last night, although it seemed cold enough inside the bag to freeze them anyway. An icicle-like frost covered the portion of the bag where I had been exhaling. Last night's low was ten degrees.

I put on my ice-cube cycling shoes and pedaled a mile to a restaurant serving breakfast. Heat is a good thing. As I waited in line to be seated, a nice young woman began asking about my trip. I carefully attempted to answer, trying not to directly breathe my caribou breath on her. Cold nights and mornings are not conducive to toothbrushing.

Ended up having a two-hour breakfast with Robin, a very nice person who works in advertising for Hewlett-Packard and is involved with the Idaho Conservation League, and her hard-charging MBA buddy, Annie, a marketing director for Women's Challenge, an Idaho touring bike race that attracts the world's best women cyclists. Nice conversation with two quality people.

Ran into Pat and Jean Ridle, owners of Middle Fork Rivers Expeditions, as I gulped down a can of spaghetti in front of the town grocery store. We talked of whitewater rafting, conservation, and the changes they've seen in Stanley over the last twenty years.

Scooted out of Stanley and lasted twenty miles before the trout gods beckoned me to the Salmon River south of town. Missed one fish. Recent cold weather really reduced insect-trout activity. A fine wade of a beautiful trout stream, nonetheless.

Unintelligently began the trek up Galena Pass at 6:00 P.M. Crawled up the steep parts at 6.5 miles per hour, watching the valley below and surrounding mountains from better views as each mile passed.

Mountain pass signs don't really give you the full story. Here are my translations:

1. "Chains recommended from this point forward."

Translation: "You will soon experience prolonged shortness of breath and an intense burning sensation in your quads—put on your game face, baby."

Steelhead and salmon reach the upper Salmon River drainage near Stanley after traveling some 900 miles from the Pacific Ocean.

2. "Trucks check your brakes—steep 6-percent grade for next eight miles."

Translation: "It's Miller time, put on a windbreaker and enjoy the nature show."

As I reached the cold summit at 8,700 feet after 2,700 feet of climbing, my bearded savior appeared and said, "Man, it looks like you could use a beer."

"Hell, yes brother," I replied to a complete classic named Joe who was hauling a '68 camper behind a Suburban. Earlier he had passed me in the middle of my climb and he must have thought, "Good God, that guy looks pathetic hauling all that crap. I think he needs a beer." Mercifully, he had hung out at the summit for twenty-five minutes to serve me a cold pilsner.

With all the hoopla, the fishing, the climb, reaching the summit, bonding with a cool dude, and indulging in a cocktail, I hadn't realized I probably wasn't in the most enviable of positions. The sun and temperature were falling fast. I was cold and I had a nippy little descent in front of me. I made a meeting plan with Joe for a couple thousand feet below, threw on some clothes, and plunged into a deep freeze that rivaled last night. At one point I reached a plateau and had to literally force my frozen legs to bend and pedal.

As planned, Joe placed a white door mat in the road at the two-track he had turned onto with his camper. My frozen eyeballs missed it in my high-speed descent, adding another two miles of wind chill to my ride. We finally connected and immediately started a large "white man fire" at our cozy campsite at 7,200 feet.

He turned into my camp mommy, serving me hot chicken noodle soup, hot chocolate, and some funky chopped pork slab over the fire. We exchanged philosophies around the campfire for about three hours, and I found this guy to be a stud—a mechanical engineering type, but creative and funny, too. We talked of the concept of marriage, the physics of fly fishing,

and the ten thousand mechanical inventions this guy
had brewing inside his skull.

Crashed in his camper—soft mattress, warm air.

LESSON: Be aware. People enter your life at
certain moments to teach you lessons, guide
you, or generally save your ass.

Day 16

Random Acts
of Kindness
[September 27]

Woke up toasty warm in Joe's Galena Hilton. I headed
out to my frosty bike and frozen water bottles and thew
on every piece of clothing I owned. Joe still had a half
day left of his four-day weekend, so we organized a
rendezvous at 10 A.M. in Sun Valley—twenty-five miles
away.

Wonderful ride following the Big Wood River. I
watched the river's progression from a dribbling brook
to a nicely flowing river as it absorbed more and more
feeder creeks.

Stopped at a small store and talked with a down-
to-earth, sassy Australian named Lorraine who had
traveled the world by crewing on yachts.

Arrived at my designated rendezvous spot with
Joe in Sun Valley, but a hefty headwind took the fun
out of my pleasant downhill journey and forced me to
arrive late. Joe was nowhere to be found, and I felt a
knot in my gut. We hadn't exchanged addresses and

The Big Wood
River, a beautiful
freestone stream,
begins in the
Boulder Moun-
tains north of
Ketchum and
runs 40 miles
south to Magic
Reservoir.

now I would never be able to buy him a cold thank-you beer or contact him in the future.

Found Ketchum to be very friendly. As I entered town, passing cars would slow down to ask my final destination or make fun of my massive load. Dropped my bike off at a small bike shop for a quick tune-up and walked around Ketchum to get a feel for the place.

A stretch of the upper Big Wood River, north of Sun Valley, ID.

I had a heartfelt conversation with a young woman named Heidi at a fancy fly shop. We both had tears well up as she told me of her mountaineering adventures on Mt. McKinley and losing one of her fellow guides to the mountain. I was able to absorb her unique perspective as a female guide and the challenges of leading and baby-sitting a group of clients, usually comprised of older men who at times were a little too proud or stubborn to heed the advice of a woman the age of their daughters.

I trolled into an organic juice shop and met a guy named Peter who appointed himself my tour guide for the remainder of the afternoon. He was a cyclist himself and had a huge heart.

I met the unique owner of the store, Anonka, a pigtailed, lean, ripped-up vegetarian who at fifty-three looked about thirty-five. He had once roller-bladed from Ketchum to Boise in eight hours and was pulled over by the police for reaching a speed of forty miles per hour. He was a practicing Hindu and had a very peaceful, calm way about him.

Peter and Anonka wanted to make sure I met a guy named Steve, a cycling guru who completed a trans-America ride in nine days, sometimes pedaling twenty-two hours in a day. We missed him at the health food shop where he worked.

I then began a run in which I was a recipient of multiple acts of random kindness: Anonka wouldn't let me pay for the awesome twelve-veggie juice he made for me; the bicycle shop insisted my tune-up was complimentary; Peter rode with me to a great trail that headed from Ketchum all the way to the town of Bellevue; and when I dined farther south in Hailey, the cool waiter I had been talking with brought me a free Caesar salad. When Peter and I bid farewell in Ketchum, I expressed my gratitude and amazement for the kindness and generosity I had received on this trip thus far. He said, "Hey, you're doing something special and people just want to be a part of it."

Spent the night tucked out of the wind next to an old church in Hailey under a dusting of snow.

The Nature Conservancy Preserve on Silver Creek, near Ketchum, offers some of the country's best catch-and-release dry fly fishing for wild trout, primarily rainbows.

LESSON: Realize that random shootings in churches and schools in America receive massive media attention and challenge our confidence in human nature, but they are far outweighed by sincere, genuine random acts of kindness that occur millions of times each day in the U.S. and often go completely unnoticed by anyone other than the recipient.

Day 17

Moonrise
[September 28]

Packed my gear in the brisk morning air and headed to a fifties-style diner to eat breakfast and thaw out.

After stoking up the furnace, I was back on the bike and following the Wood River Trail to Bellevue.

Crossed paths with a couple more classics. One was a crusty river guide who was power washing his drift boat in preparation for a twenty-day float of the Grand Canyon. A tinge of envy overcame me as he gave me the tour of his vessel. As we shook hands and wished each other luck, he told me of a hot springs on my way to Craters of the Moon in Arco. The other classic was a bearded businessman who shared a few memories of his hitchhiking across America twenty years ago.

It was a continual source of mystery to me how I was able to cross paths with so many unique people in a day despite spending 95 percent of my time riding, fly fishing, or camping in unpopulated areas. And it seemed the conversations I did have quickly leapt past the usual insignificant babbling and moved into something deeper. Many times, people struck up conversations not to hear anything I had to say but to share with me a similar fishing, cycling, hiking, or breaking-away experience. Good shit.

Honest, man, that hog was this big.

Twenty miles into today's journey the seductive call of the river goddess once again thrashed my plans for a 100-mile day. Crossing a small creek I spotted an eight-inch rainbow rising near the gravel bank, and then in an adjacent run I spotted his sixteen-inch big brother...and another. Cycle schmycle. This whole trip is called Riding for Rivers—remember, Jeff.

Decided to give it a shot, especially since I had seen no bug activity since the recent cold snap. Good call. Since it was a small, shallow creek, I blew off wearing my waders and just quickly threw on my wading boots. Bad call.

Hiked three-quarters of a mile downstream, keeping well away from the bank and the fish's view, yet close enough to spot a few more rises. Trout fever, baby. Began fishing upstream and initially brought up a good fish with a hopper, but a hatch of medium-sized brown mayflies led me to tie on a size 12 Adams. I hooked and landed a fat eighteen-inch brown. Gorgeous fish. I couldn't feel my legs anymore. The tiny little creek had me wading up to my waist in cycling shorts, and although the spring-fed water was good for my sore legs, it sucked the warmth out of me.

A second hatch began and my trembling hand barely threaded the hook as I tied on a smaller Adams. I was fortunate to hook a beautifully spotted sixteen-inch rainbow and then a smaller bow. Total damage to cycling time: four hours. Ouch.

Decided I would have to pedal into the evening if I were to cover any distance today. Climbed a hill into Carey and stopped at a convenience store. As I consumed a gourmet meal of canned lasagna and tuna, I spoke with a wonderful lady in a camouflage coat who rolled her eyes when I told her I was heading to Arco tonight.

I reached the hot springs just after sunset and did a quick mental calculation: (wet hair from hot springs) + (riding bike into headwind with lows of twenty degrees tonight) = (Jeff not the sharpest tool in the shed).

The warm water was too much to resist. I whipped off all my clothes and eased into the steamy water, which was amazingly clear and the perfect temperature. As I soaked my sore back and legs, I released the frigid flashbacks of today's fishing excursion. It was difficult remembering that this was not a man-made luxury device. It was definitely a gift from God. I toyed with the idea of camping here for the night so I could awake and enjoy a natural Jacuzzi, but I had miles to cover and dismissed the temptation as weak and undisciplined.

I pressed on in the dark along the desolate highway and charged up the 1,100-foot climb to Craters of the Moon. It was a little disappointing. I couldn't see

The strange lunar landscape of Craters of the Moon National Monument was created by fissure vents, volcanic cones, and lava flows of the Great Rift zone. Eruptions started 15,000 years ago and ceased only 2,000 years ago. Geologists expect the landscape to erupt again. To the south of the park lies the vast Craters of the Moon Wilderness.

clearly the mysterious-looking lava flows of the area, but the ride in the dark was eerie enough. At one point a vehicle approached me from behind and its lights quickly flashed on a tall shrub two feet from the road that appeared just like a human form charging me. WWWHHOOOOOAAAA!

As I reached the summit, I noticed several faint streaks of light along the horizon. I thought it must be from Arco twenty-five miles away. Seconds later the tip of a monstrous orange moon exposed itself—awesome sight. I bundled up in every piece of clothing I owned and enjoyed a mesmerizing ride staring at the moon and stars. I watched the progression of the rising moon change from bright orange to pale orange to yellow and finally to white as it rose high in the sky.

I had Galena Pass flashbacks as I pedaled hard the final twenty miles—the keyword here being wind chill. Reached Arco with great expectations of warm all-night diners or truck stops but found only a small town that was extremely dormant by my midnight arrival.

Found a park and lit my Trangia cookstove in a feeble attempt to thaw my hands and feet. I made a couple of delicious batches of boiling water and honey, gulped them down, and snuck into my cozy sleeping bag.

LESSON: Strong, clear callings from the river goddess should never be ignored.

Messing with Mother Nature

[September 29]

This needed to be a blue-collar day. Arco was not the most picturesque city, with its mountain backdrop plastered with the scribbling of twenty year's worth of drunken graduating high-school classes. Arco prided itself as the first city in the world to receive power from atomic energy.

I wore my baseball cap down over my sunglasses and rode hard for fifty-eight miles until I reached Blackfoot. I pumped hard into a brisk wind that made it feel like I was cycling in mud. In Arco I had discovered from the locals that a couple of days ago they had winds gusting to fifty miles per hour across the desert-like plains. So, I merely note this headwind—I'm not complaining!

Throughout my ride across Washington and Idaho, I was amazed the way irrigation had transformed dry, ugly barren land into lush fields. On a bicycle you really are aware of the contrast between the dusty desert and the moist green fields immediately adjacent to it. It doesn't feel natural. I get a weird feeling in my stomach thinking of the consequences of the well-intentioned action that supports our working farmers.

My topographical map showed I crossed no contour lines, but I pumped up (and down) at least twelve one- or two-mile climbs of 100 feet or so. That's the element of surprise you get when you have a map with contour intervals of 500 feet.

I arrived in Blackfoot and talked with a rambunctious Wendy's staff. As I left, the manager, Brady, presented me with a few ten-dollar gift certificates compliments of his boss. Can you say, "Building a lifetime customer"? I thought that was great.

Rode along a twenty-mile stretch down loud and busy Interstate 15—definitely not my style. I cut my ride short so I could pick up a care package from my girlfriend, Julia, tomorrow morning at the Pocatello post office.

Found a school soccer field, laid out my tarp, gazed at the stars, and thought tired cyclist thoughts.

LESSON: It's not nice to fool with Mother Nature. Good intentions and well-engineered systems applied upstream have negative impacts on the complex web of life downstream.

Day 19

Playground Pervert
[September 30]

Pulled my bivy sack from over the top of my head and saw it was quite light. Through my squinting eyes I spotted a couple of little girls moving along a crosswalk toward my crude campground. I'd better hustle.

Within the ten minutes it took me to ready my gear, the schoolyard was bustling with 150 students. Two cautious teachers were acting like riot police to hold them back from checking out the curious guy with the bike in the playground. I strategically slid behind a large tree as I slipped into my bike shorts and then quickly located my panniers under the inquisitive stares of a playground full of students.

I rode up to the teachers in an effort to explain my ride and, I hoped, demonstrate that I wasn't a complete freak of nature. They laughed as we spoke and we were soon surrounded by all the students.

I said we were doing updates of the ride on the Internet and tried to snap a quick picture of the hordes of students around us. One of the teachers, in a teacher kind of way, scolded me and said that she couldn't allow pictures of children on the Internet. Being reprimanded by teachers is nothing new to me. I high-fived a couple of boys as I jumped on my bike, and the weird guy attempting to exploit young children left the playground and rode into the sunrise.

Scooted around downtown Pocatello, waited for the post office to open, and collected my package of muffins (now moldy) from Julia. Whoops. So I'm a little behind schedule. By the time I worked my way out of town, it was close to eleven. I headed east out of town on Buckskin Road, partly because I wanted to avoid the noise, traffic, and stress of Interstate 15, but mostly because it sounded like a "manly" road. My shortcut rose 1,500 feet within a few miles and somewhat humbled me. Suddenly, the noise and traffic of I-15 seemed a little more attractive.

Part of the way into the descent, Rapid Creek Road turned to gravel, allowing me to ram my skinny wheel rims into some hidden potholes. I came upon a group of twenty horses that were drinking out of Rapid Creek, and I noticed there was not a fence between them and the road. My bumpy rambling down the hill must have been muffled by the sound of the stream because as I approached two or three of the horses standing in the creek completely spooked. Their heads popped up and they lurched, completely freaking out the rest of the herd. A couple bolted near the road, but fortunately I missed them.

Talked with a very nice man in Inkom. He gave me route advice, utilizing all four of his teeth to form his words. I jumped back on I-15 for ten miles and geared down, taking whatever the headwind gave me. I cranked it up during brief calm spells and then backed off during gusts.

I stopped at a gas station on State Road 30 and had a macho conversation staring straight ahead at the urinal with a fellow fly fisherman. As I planted myself outside the store's door to rest and eat, a young man who had passed me on the highway came by. "Nice effort," he said, as he threw me a banana he had purchased.

Outside of Lava Hot Springs I was blessed with a tail wind that helped push me up a 1,600-foot climb to Fish Creek Summit at 6,000 feet. I knew those ugly, wind-blocking panniers were good for something. Truly enjoyed the descent since, finally, I wasn't beginning it at night in thirty-degree weather. I shot down into a huge bowl called Alexander Crater surrounded by mountains. The crater was roughly eleven miles by thirty miles, and it was filled completely with beautiful farmland.

Completed my ride in the dark to Soda Springs to meet Julia for a weekend of R & R. I guess I need to change my wool-blend socks that have been my constant companion over the last eight days.

LESSON: State and federal officials place highways in the most topographically efficient corridors. Backroads are backroads for a reason.

Warp Speed
[October 1]

You'd think my first night inside after three weeks would be characterized by wonderful warmth and complete restfulness. Instead, the air seemed stagnant and I felt a little claustrophobic.

We ditched my bike in a storage room at the hotel, threw my panniers into the trunk of our rental car, and headed back toward Ketchum.

Very strange day for several reasons:

1. I didn't have that comfortable layer of road grunge and stink covering my body anymore.

2. I had a day of constant conversation and joking with Julia instead of listening to my own uninterrupted self-talk for sixteen hours.

3. I wasn't forced to strategize about water stops, food stops, and route decisions.

4. We sped in a car for two-and-one-half hours over a route that took me four days to cover on the bike. I freaked out at the minimal length of time it took our vehicle to climb the hills I had labored over. From the passenger side at seventy miles per hour, I was mesmerized by the endless white line I was used to following at fifteen miles per hour.

5. My legs were in disbelief that I wasn't hammering them for eight hours.

6. I was able to ditch those tight, constricting, nonventilating, odor-retaining, invented-by-a-male-hating-female-engineer biking shorts for a loose pair of casual shorts.

We stopped for a quick dip at the hot springs I had visited previously near Craters of the Moon and were treated with an unrequested strip show by a friendly, fun-loving couple. Why is it that those you wish would keep their clothes on tend to disrobe, and those you wouldn't mind taking a more unencumbered gawk at keep covered?

Julia with a nice rainbow near Ketchum, Idaho.

We dressed Julia up in my oversized waders and boots and went after a few rainbows and browns. Julia battled the wind initially but then was delighted when a light midge hatch started and the wind turned from gale force to merely brisk. We lightened up to 7X tippets to match the tiny hatching bugs, and Julia hooked a nice rainbow as the bright orange sun set.

Grubbed on wonderful Italian food and indulged in a bottle of wine that seemed to manhandle both of us lightweights. Hmmm. Must be the altitude.

We crashed in the tent pitched in a field near Hailey.

LESSON: It is comforting to be truly content and grounded when you are alone for extended periods of time, but the joys in life become amplified when you can share them with someone you care about.

At Play iN SuN Valley

[October 2]

We woke up to an officer of the Hailey Gun Club inquiring if we had a restful night's sleep and requesting that we promptly remove our tent so they could begin preparation in the shooting range for a gun safety class. Whoops. The downside of finding a campsite at night.

Played in Ketchum most of the day, running into the same cast of characters that I had encountered a few days before: Peter, the big-hearted, unsolicited tour guide and his three-legged dog; Anonka, the shredded Hindu juice guy…

Fished late in the afternoon, once again just in time for the winds to hit their maximum velocity. It was the type of wind that could hold twenty feet of fly line parallel to the water and whip the fly about. It was actually a bit of a blessing; although placing the fly was difficult, the wind roughed up the once-smooth creek surface and allowed us to make our presentations without putting the spooky rainbows on guard.

Julia hooked three fish, one a beautifully colored fifteen-inch rainbow. I get so much more excitement from watching a trout rise to her fly than I do from any fish I hook. After a couple of hours of playing guide, I ripped the rod from Julia's hands and watched the trout gods shake their angry heads at my selfishness. Six beautiful fish rose for my fly; I landed none.

We were spoiled by Jim, the host of the Pioneer Saloon, and indulged in a great steak. I followed a pretty wholesome vegetarian diet for a year prior to this ride, but there's something about biking your buns off that prompts you to consume food with the highest possible sugar and fat content.

Lesson: It's wonderful watching women cast a fly rod. They don't try to overpower the rod with strength alone; they cast effectively by using flawless, graceful form.

Day 22

The Meaning of Luck
[October 3]

I took some of the load out of my panniers and put it into Julia's duffel bag in an attempt to transform my touring bicycle from a heavy Gold Wing cruiser with a side car into merely a Harley Davidson Fat Boy.

Took a nice little hike with Julia along the Big Wood River, spooking a trout or two. We were taking our final stroll down Ketchum's main street when we came upon two beautiful yellow Labs in the cab of a truck. We laughed as one brought its saliva-soaked teddy bear to the truck window for us to check out.

The dog's owner headed out of the nearby fly shop and busted us peering into his truck cab and gawking at his cool dogs. As we struck up a conversation with him, my old pal Heidi, the McKinley mountaineer, dashed out of the shop.

These were her dogs...and her husband. It's strange when you are overcome with an easy, comfortable feeling around some complete strangers, as though you know them.

As usual, we were on the verge of making Julia late for her flight out of Salt Lake City, so I jumped behind the wheel and within minutes was having another fascinating conversation with another friendly stranger—a state policeman. I think I'm sticking to bicycles.

I analyzed the topo maps for my route through Colorado, Kansas, Missouri, Tennessee, and Georgia while the lighter-footed Julia drove. I became queasy as I squinted at the small print while my partner managed to hit every bump in rural Idaho.

Now, looking at the Idaho map, I calculated that Julia was cutting it very close on making her flight, so instead of dropping me off in Soda Springs and backtracking to Salt Lake, I suggested she just drop me off at a gas station at the intersection of I-15 and U.S. 30; then I would hitchhike to my bike in Soda Springs and save her an entire hour. She reluctantly agreed, and I immediately began scouting for the perfect ride—a person who looked halfway clean-cut and respectable, but earthy enough to pick up a dirt bag like me.

It took me only five minutes to find a rugged-looking guy with a Fu Man-chu mustache and an old Toyota truck that was meticulously packed for a hunting trip. I asked if he was heading east and he reluctantly agreed to let me join him. As he made room in his truck for me, he strategically let me get a view of the handgun between the seats, just to enlighten me with the fact that he would have no hesitation in whacking me if I attempted anything crazy—though he later denied this.

I was fortunate to share this ride with another classic. His name was Jack Spencer and his business card labeled him as a biologist, trapper, and aerial gunner. He was trained as a wildlife biologist and worked for a wildlife management service trapping and shooting coyotes that were a menace to area ranchers.

After he conducted an in-depth biological analysis of an area's coyote population, he would remedy the situation by trapping and relocating or shooting the coyotes from a small plane. I cautiously noted Aldo Leopold's web of life arguments, and he responded

Aldo Leopold's book, "A Sand County Almanac," was first published in 1949 and is a classic work of American nature writing that provides the core of modern conservation ethics.

genuinely, describing how he walked the thin line between economics and wildlife preservation.

Got back to Soda Springs, shook hands with Jack,
grabbed my bike, and slipped my grungy wool socks
back on. I biked two blocks to the thermal geyser in
town to eat a sandwich and watch the show.

I ran into one of the most unique people of the
trip. The thermal park was empty and a seventy-six-
year-old guy in a red wool jacket walked up to me and
proceeded to correctly guess the contents and location
of everything I had in my panniers. At this point, his
daughter (or was it his girlfriend?) walked away, fully
aware from experience that a lengthy conversation was
about to unfold. I told him about my bike ride, and he
described how at sixteen years of age he ran away from
home in Utah, hitchhiked to San Diego, snuck onto a
military plane heading to Panama, and spent the next
three months finding his way back home.

He worked as a rancher in Utah until his wife died,
and he then began furthering his college education,
eventually earning a master's degree in mechanical
engineering and astrophysics. His daughter/girlfriend
returned from the forty-foot spouting geyser to fill in
a few more details. As we parted he said, "I wish you
good luck. And remember, you spell luck, W-O-R-K."

I headed down the road fifteen miles or so, contemplating all the while everything the old man had
said. My reverie was interrupted when some yahoo in
a passing car stuck his head and torso out of the window three feet from me and yelled, "Heeeeeeey!" It
was the old man wildly waving his hands.

I pointed my bike south to the small town of
Georgetown where I met a wonderful couple taking a
stroll. I learned that they had been married sixty-two
years, and as we talked, the husband became slightly
preoccupied, glancing periodically at my bike. Eventually he asked, "Now you've got something on that
bike that propels you, right?"

"Yeah, Pop-Tarts," I told him.

Checked my voicemail in Montpelier and had two messages from Julia. The first came from a rest area on her way to the plane; she made fun of me for hitch-hiking since she had plenty of time, noting that my time-distance calculations sucked. The second came informing me that her hateful attempt to chastise me with the call from the rest area resulted in a flat tire for her (bad karma) and she barely made her flight.

After only three hours of pedaling, I stopped at sunset in a field of fresh-cut hay. I collected piles of hay, formed a foot-deep bed, laid out my tarp and sleeping bag, and passed out under the stars.

LeSSON: I wish you all good luck, and remember, you spell luck W-O-R-K.

Day 23

Driving for Swine; Thinking about Cows
[October 4]

It is now time for the "DRIVE FOR THE SWINE." I need to put the hammer down to reach Salida, Colorado, by October 7 for the Pig Roast and Fly Fishing Extravaganza at Matty Brown's shack on the Arkansas River.

I made nice time in the morning, quickly covering thirty miles to the town of Cokeville, Wyoming. I went from battling a stinging cold face and frozen snot in my nose at 7:30 A.M. to a shirtless climb up Border Summit at 10 A.M.

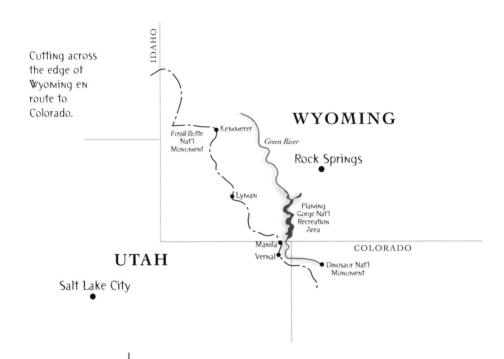

Cutting across
the edge of
Wyoming en
route to
Colorado.

IDAHO

WYOMING

Fossil Butte
Nat'l
Monument

Kemmerer

Green River

Rock Springs

Lyman

Flaming
Gorge Nat'l
Recreation
Area

Manila

Vernal

COLORADO

UTAH

Dinosaur Nat'l
Monument

Salt Lake City

I spent four hours on the phone handling administrative tasks and updating my journal, and suddenly it was 3 P.M. and I had only covered thirty miles. Hmmm.

I pedaled hard through fifty-five miles of sagebrush and jackrabbits until I reached Kemmerer. Near Fossil Butte National Monument a ruthless and cagey canine made a slight error by growling three seconds too early from beneath his bushy ambush spot, and I was able to outrun the dirty jackal after a tenth of a mile.

Since I was facing forty-two miles of road without the prospect of food and water, I was forced to leave the highway and head two miles downhill to Kemmerer and then crawl two miles back out after grabbing supplies. I pedaled until 9 P.M., surprised to find few gusts of warm air.

I didn't grow up on a farm, but I think my current case study of over two thousand cows throughout the three states of Washington, Idaho, and Wyoming gives me enough credibility to present the following theory.

I've watched approximately 150 times as one cow begins to run or walk in a certain direction. It either got stung in the butt by a bee or, for no particular reason at all, its feeble cow brain said "Run."

Without exception, at least twenty cows will follow this clueless, directionless cow—not because this poop-smeared, brawny animal is an exceptional leader that has new insights, has a well-thought-out agenda, or is just a quality cow, but just because it is swiftly moving in a specific direction.

As independent, thoughtful humans we can laugh at this mindless and unsophisticated behavior—but we shouldn't. You and I engage in it daily. Rarely do any of us carve out a unique existence from the unremitting flow of expectations and subtle directives fed to us by television, magazines, family, and friends. Rarely do we dedicate the time and energy needed to probe our true feelings and set a unique course of action based on them. Instead we follow the cow in front of us, buying up silly Beanie Babies and driving shiny SUVs that never leave pavement.

LESSON: Work hard at not being a cow.

Fossil Butte National Monument preserves the site where Fossil Lake once stood 50 million years ago. The fossils preserved here—including many large predatory fish—are among the most nearly perfect preserved remains of ancient plant and animal life.

Just Runnin'
Against the Wind
[October 5]

Arose on the twenty-fourth day of sunshine in a row in a dusty field eighty yards off County Road 412.

Early morning cycling has usually been pretty relaxing because my rickety old football body is not up to the task of cranking hard up hills until it becomes properly lubricated at about ten in the morning. I have also eased the bike through the descents early in the day so that I don't have to ice-pick the snot icicles off my lip.

After eight miles of pedaling arrived at the dot on the map that was supposed to be the town of Carter, but instead I found three run-down buildings and a dusty dog. Cranked another fifteen miles to the town of Mountain View, raided another grocery store, and sat happily on its sunny sidewalk munching away.

I became an easy target for the three deli ladies who left for their lunch breaks in fifteen-minute intervals. I happened to still be there eating as each of them finished their forty-minute lunch, and they each independently said, "Well, it looks like you're not getting very far."

Talked with another fly fishing guide whose home turf is the Green River. He whined a bit about having to deal with arrogant clients now and again, and I promptly reminded him that he is able to contend with difficult clients under the sun on a beautiful river while the rest of America's business people do it in stuffy offices wearing monkey suits.

I traveled mostly south today, directly into the face

of a stiff wind. During my thirty-four-mile ride from Mountain View to McKinnon, the moody Cycling Gods threw in a 1,100-foot climb just to add a little extra challenge. I tried to take whatever the wind would give, but it would give little, if anything.

Arrived at the dot on the map that was supposed to be the town of McKinnon (and a cold beverage). Instead it was a church and a 300-foot climb. I relaxed with a cold can of "taco pasta and beef" from my panniers and was amazed how close its consistency and flavor was to Alpo beef parts.

As I rallied south of McKinnon, I was treated to some wonderful scenery under a pink-orange sun, the beautiful valleys reaching toward Flaming Gorge National Recreation Area. During my ride today it appeared at times as though I was barely moving. Every bend in the road facing south put me nose to nose with the wind. But without exception, if I sucked it up in low gear for fifteen minutes...or an hour...the direction of the road would change and allow me to cruise comfortably. Or I would come across a sweet stretch of scenery that would turn things around, wind or no wind.

The 91-mile long Lake Flaming Gorge was created in 1963 with the completion of the Flaming Gorge Dam on the Green River.

Battled hills and a leaky tire for this sweet view of Flaming Gorge Reservoir.

Near Manila, UT

LESSON: Periods of toil that appear to have no end are always followed by brighter times in which your spirits rise. So why waste your time with energy-sucking negativism in the first place.

Character Building

[October 6]

Up to this point I have been blessed with two huge pieces of good luck: (1) twenty-four straight days of sunshine and (2) no mechanical problems whatsoever. And up to this point I've tried hard not to mention it very often so as not to jinx myself. This morning I spouted off on a radio show in Grand Junction, Colorado—going on and on about my streak of luck. Hmmm.

I pedaled out of Manila, Utah, into the first steep climb that had me wondering why I was expending so much energy. Then I noticed my rear tire was flat. I investigated and found it was a slow leak, so I decided to just refill it using my hand pump and keep pedaling. The decision was driven partially because the leak wasn't that bad and partially because the scenery was sweet and I was antsy to cover some ground.

Mule deer on a Utah hillside. South of Manila, UT

I was treated to some unbelievable views of Flaming Gorge and the beautiful sandstone formations that blended from creamy tan to deep brick red. I rode within twenty feet of a group of mule deer on a rocky hillside; they just watched peacefully as I passed. I crossed crystal-clear Sheep Creek after a 600-foot climb and fully realized how fortunate I was to be able to slowly (very slowly) explore such beautiful country.

I then began the character-building portion of the day. After a magical downhill, smelling sagebrush and feeling the warm air, I began a tough 1,500-foot uphill into a strong wind. It was the kind of wind where gusts tip you back on your heels. I was heading due south virtually the entire day, directly into the gelatinous belly of this fat wind. I experienced a two-mile stretch in which I cranked up a 6-percent grade into this wall of wind. My bike computer showed I was moving at 3.5 mph, but only because that is the lowest velocity increment. I believe it was closer to 1 mph.

I think it's healthy to be presented with these moments in life in which you feel completely frustrated and helpless. I was pedaling as hard as I could, but I was moving at slower than walking pace and realized that this wind was going to be my companion the remainder of the day. For me, these momentary feelings of self-pity are followed by a realization that I'm being a sissy; then I get angry with myself and become determined to work hard.

I continued filling my slow leak during my breaks from riding. During one filling session, I kneeled in the grass along the shoulder and spotted a fresh bobcat road kill staring up at me. I climbed a total of 3,500 feet over sixty-two miles, hurrying to arrive at the 8,500-foot summit and begin my descent before it became dark and cold. The sandstone scenery gave way to dark evergreens, sprinkled with bright yellow aspen.

I reached the summit and began a descent that contained ten sharp switchbacks over nine miles. Descents are always a wonderful reward for your climbing efforts, but this one contained a special lightning show about twenty miles in the distance to complement the effortless 30-mph coast. I continued into the dark reaching Vernal, Utah, and feeling spent. I found an isolated field, constructed a quick rain cover utilizing my tarp and a barbed wire fence, and weathered out a blustery, rainy night.

63

LesSON: The optimal response to helplessness, frustration, and temporary self-pity is determination and hard work.

Day 26

A Time for Swine
[October 7]

Woke up damp and feeling a bit used up. Successfully held back a barf session in the morning (I needed the calories) as I worked on my rear tire. I patched the tire in three places rather than put in a new tube, not only because I'm cheap but because I was emotionally attached to the tire and tube I dunked in Puget Sound a few miles ago. Felt pretty awful as I cycled into downtown Vernal and grabbed some breakfast.

As I parked my bike, a man and his wife spent a few minutes talking with me and the man described how he attempted to ride from Canada to Mexico ten years ago. He ended up quitting after 1,000 miles because the cycling grind and weather drove his morale down. As I continued to restrain my puke, even more difficult as I heard his story, I vowed to not let it happen to me.

In order to recover, I was forced to head to the grassy hospital grounds for a quick nap under a tree. I felt halfway decent after an hour and headed to a nearby bike shop and met a great guy working there. We talked biking as he laughed at my bald rear tire. As we spoke, he drew parallels to the way his fifteen-year-old crickity Lab and I walked. As I left, two young high-school girls gave me a ten-minute description of what they do for fun in the town of Vernal, making me feel fortunate I slept several miles north of town.

I fell about three days shy of hitting my target date in Salida for the Roasting of the Swine, so I searched for a car rental shop in order meet my buddies arriving tonight. The owner of Utah Motors took me under his wing, showed me some flies his son had tied, allowed me to store my bike in the back of his showroom, and hooked me up with the cheapest, dirtiest vehicle he had.

It gave me a strange sensation as I drove toward Salida on the cycling route I would take a few days after our get-together. I really did not like scouting the terrain, knowing what the exact elevation changes were, knowing what the small in-between towns looked like, and feeling my mechanically unsound vehicle repeatedly jerk into low gear as I traveled along the mountainous roads. My legs twitched each time I headed up a steep pass, feeling the car labor up the steep grades. Anticipating events with preconceived notions of them—or, in this case, the actual prior experience of the event—robs us from truly experiencing those events.

Arrived in Salida at twilight still feeling woozy but excited to see all the boys. One by one they arrived at Browner's Guide Service, and one by one the frosty beers flowed. As the crew arrived, each independently pressed his face against the kitchen window announcing his arrival. When it came time for Charlie Thompson to arrive, our buddy Starky could not contain his enthusiasm. He rushed the window, unintentionally breaking the glass into Charlie's face, doing minimal damage to Charlie but setting the tone for an entertaining weekend.

LESSON: Preconceived notions of future events subtly destroy the spontaneity and true experience of those events.

Caution: Young Boys at Play

[October 8]

Outstanding day today, especially in contrast to the headaches and nausea of yesterday. We all descended upon a small cafe for breakfast, catching up on life and inhaling all-you-can-eat pancakes and eggs. The Browner brothers organized a top-notch float down the Arkansas River and donated all the proceeds to my Riding for Rivers fundraiser. Classy move.

We took off for a five-hour float looking like a bunch of excited kids on a playground. We were fired up to hook some brown trout, enjoy the beautiful Arkansas River valley, and harass each other regarding our latest girlfriends. The action was sweet. We started stripping black Woolly Buggers and immediately began hooking thirteen- to fifteen-inch browns.

What a great feeling it is to get into the zone, concentrating hard on making as many quality casts as possible as you float through prime water, witnessing trout chase your fly, feeling the thump as they pound it, giving them a smooch as you release them back into the clear water. Another sunny, cloudless day, another example of grown men acting like excitable young boys.

Stripping streamers on the Arkansas River under the watchful eye of guide Brown Dog

Salida, CO

Matt Brown, during his busy season, unfortunately is not able to properly feed his fly fishing addiction, so it was enjoyable watching him fish as Mark Snyder worked the oars. He worked a size 16 Blue-winged Olive like a master, covering huge amounts of water and traversing complicated currents with the small dry fly. Fly fishing is truly a marriage of the spiritual and the technical. The beautiful, poetic, artful motions of the fly line combine with precise techniques and space-age fly rod materials.

We ended the float at the Browners' fly shop and home on the river. Sometimes life is too easy. We tossed the football around — a handful of old, washed-up college football and basketball players who still feel like they could suit up on Saturday if they had to. It was good being with the fellas. Took off during the festivities to drive to Colorado Springs to pick up Julia at the airport, also a good thing.

LESSON: It seems to me that a large part of grown men's being is still playful and child-like. They are still boys. One of the tricks to living well is to retain those positive emotions and still use our rational, adult side to prevent us from becoming merely childish.

The Arkansas River rises in central Colorado's Sawatch Range and flows for 1,460 miles to the Mississippi River. Unlike many Colorado rivers, it travels more than 150 miles from its headwaters until it encounters a dam in Pueblo on Colorado's eastern plains. Under the guidance of anglers and rafters, the headwaters is recovering as a first-class river.

Day 28

River Dogs
[October 9]

I snuck out with Julia early in the morning to do a quick wade and fish before the pig roast festivities started in early afternoon. We had a nice time working the pocket water near shore, picking up a couple of browns, but we didn't hammer them like the day

utah

before. Must have been the cool, bright morning conditions. It couldn't have been our fault.

Matty Brown and the boys had the full party spread prepared by the time we arrived. Fantastic time as we ate, drank, and burped ourselves silly from two in the afternoon until two in the morning. We partied right on the sunny river, gorging ourselves on perfectly cooked

Buffoonery on the Arkansas.

Salida, CO

swine and mingling with the Salida natives. We reunited with our buddy Stretch, a talented rock climber who just successfully scaled Yosemite's El Capitan with his partner Adam. Also met a poor soul with an incurable case of trout fever, fifty-year-old Chuck Pine who shared his classic trout lore until he literally slid off his picnic table seat. The stories, river games, and Big Head Todd tunes continued as we all enjoyed the sound of the river and the light of the bonfire. Another fantastic day with a solid crew of river dogs.

LESSON: When it truly comes down to it, family, friends, and faith are the core of our lives. Yet the majority of our energies are often directed toward other things related to our careers, businesses, or social obligations.

The Joys of Small Streams

[October 10]

We all pitched in to clean up the aftermath of twelve hours of river buffoonery. Julia and I then slipped away for a day and a half of fishing on a nearby creek. The year before we performed an exhausting twenty-six-mile hike of the entire creek, fishing and exploring the stream and canyon from 6 A.M. until 2 A.M. the next day. It was a bit torturous because we spotted plenty of fish but were forced to hike hard rather than fish in order to complete the trip.

This time we opted for the "fish more, hike less" strategy. We spotted a group of bighorn sheep camouflaged against a hillside as we started our hike. The creek was only four feet wide in some sections, and we had a fantastic time locating fourteen-inch browns and delicately presenting Royal Wulffs on 7X tippets. It was a complete rush watching the fish spot the fly in the clear, shallow water and then strike. We had one fly rod between us so we traded off landing beautiful browns and exchanging playful insults.

It is becoming a bit more difficult fly fishing with Julia. When she was first introduced to the sport a couple of years ago, she thought that every cast I made was masterful, but two years of experience have now given her the ability to recognize when I mess up. I hate it when that happens. We enjoyed a dinner of plain pasta topped with seasonings. I'm always amazed how such simple food tastes so wonderful on a backpacking trip. We enjoyed a cozy campfire, and I made sure not to reveal any more fly fishing secrets to Julia.

LESSON: Working toward simplicity in life allows you to have a deeper enjoyment of all things…friends, nature, food, conversation.

Day 30

Dead Meat
[October 11]

We packed away our frosty tent and gear so that we could combine an early morning fish with our hike out.

Julia with a sweet little trout in the backcountry.

It was one of those nippy mornings in which you tied on a fly by visually leading your fingers because your sense of feel had completely disappeared.

The cold morning did not keep the aggressive trout from attacking dry flies. Julia's first cast yielded a splashy strike. We hiked out using a slightly different route, allowing us to enjoy some sweet vistas of the creek and canyon. That goofy, empty feeling that a wonderful weekend was winding down began to set in.

For five days, the trip was flowing just a little too smoothly, with no real challenges. We were on time to get Julia to the airport as we packed our gear in the spunky little Dodge Neon. The dusty, go-cart-like vehicle looked like it was ready to handle the twenty-

ride

five-mile gravel and rock road in front of it. During a relatively steep, narrow incline, we managed to kick up a baseball-sized rock that thumped loudly underneath the floorboards. The car died immediately on the steepest part of the tree-lined road. I managed to momentarily start the car again, but it immediately stalled. We were approximately ten miles from the nearest ranch, and my knowledge of auto mechanics is only exceeded by my knowledge of male-female relationships, so we were in a bit of a bind.

The car cranked well, so I knew it was fuel-related, but we were dead meat. I was mentally preparing to start a ten-mile run when a couple of orange-hatted dudes in a truck approached. We had all the doors of our vehicle open, completely blocking the narrow passage, so they had to stop. Perhaps because we looked pitiful and harmless enough, they agreed to take us and our gear back to the fly shop. I threw the beaten car in neutral and rolled it off to the side of the road so that any other vehicle could squeak by.

We took a humorous ride with Dean and his buddy Dean, discussing the social impact of the breakup of Van Halen and helping them spot mule deer from the dirt road. We wished the Deans well, observing that our time buffer to transport Julia to the airport had rapidly disappeared. As Julia packed, I called the friendly car guys in Utah, hoping they were nice to customers even after the customers disabled their vehicles. We drove the two hours to the Colorado Springs airport in Matty's Suburban. As we walked to Julia's gate, a very strange-looking man quickly darted at me from behind a row of chairs and half tackled me. It was my identical twin brother, Brad, and he happened to be on Julia's flight.

I took a contemplative solo drive back to Salida, reminiscing about the fun-filled weekend.

LESSON: Sometimes cheap cars that act like they are up for a challenge still suck.

Itching for the Road

[October 12]

Completely overcome today by feelings of impatience and suffocation. I spent most of the day negotiating who would pay for the $283 towing bill and $90 of repairs to my scrappy little Neon, and then waiting for the work to be completed. I suppose that had I fly fished less in Idaho there would have been no need for a rental car in the first place! But we've all got our priorities.

My car ride to Salida allowed me to get a close look at the snow on the summits of the four passes I needed to climb in Colorado. I hope my string of beautiful weather continues. Matt Brown and I both left Salida at 7 P.M. I was eagerly looking forward to covering some miles and sleeping under the stars while Matt was heading to Belize to fly fish for monster tarpon and elusive permit.

I chose a different route back to Vernal, Utah, and, after I caught myself manually holding my eyelids open with my index finger and pinky, I decided to pull over near Vail to crash in my stinky little vehicle.

At three in the morning, I awoke to the bright beam of a police officer's spotlight checking out my sporty roadster. Once I popped my delirious head out of my sleeping bag, the officer realized I was just some moron sleeping in my car and that the vehicle was not abandoned, which perhaps it should have been.

LESSON: There is a balance in life between impatiently, zealously trying to complete tasks and goals and being content and enjoying where you are in life. If the scale tips too far to the impatience side, you become stressed and miserable to be around. Yet, too much contentment kills ambition.

Out of the Comfort Zone
[October 13]

I woke up to a unique blend of odors trapped inside my Neon…concentrated bad breath, human gaseous discharge, and the remnants of cigarette smoke from the other four hundred idiots who rented this car before me. If I could only have bottled a sample, I'd have a potent weapon.

I drove the remainder of the way back to Vernal, Utah, following the White River and daydreaming of having my kayak and fly rod with me to explore all its riffles and runs. I arrived at the car rental place and found the staff to be true gentlemen. They absorbed all the repair costs and didn't charge me for the extra day of rental it took to return the vehicle. Perhaps they knew from the beginning that they had rented me a real piece of work.

My emotional attachment to my bicycle's original tire tubes ended when I saw my deflated rear tire wheeled out of the storage room. I performed a quick tube replacement on the bike and was finally on the road at 1 P.M.

It was a strange feeling to be riding again. Within a day I went from laughing and joking with all of my best buddies to pedaling solo across the desert, fifty miles from anyone. Yet it was a wonderful feeling of freedom to be riding in the sunshine with only a few material possessions.

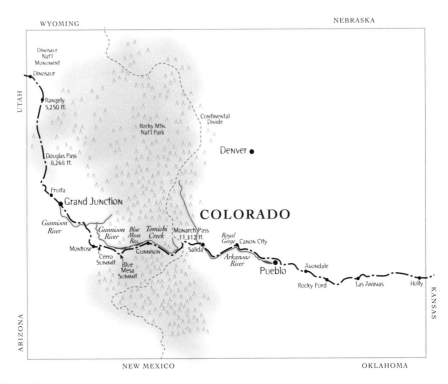

Up and over the
Continental
Divide, headed
for the flatlands.

Comfort zones suck. A week before, as I drove this exact route in my cozy, environmentally controlled rental car, I had a host of serious concerns: "Boy these hills are steep; my car can barely handle them." "It sure is a long way between water stops—seventy-three miles." "I don't really see a good place to throw my sleeping bag on this route."

When I finally was able to pedal my bike along the route, I found it a fairly easy ride. I covered sixty-nine miles in half a day, not taking much time to strike up conversations. I slept six miles south of Rangely, Colorado, at the foot of desertlike hills and fell asleep to the serenade of five howling coyotes.

ride

Lesson: Comfort zones restrict growth. The pain of moving beyond these familiar patterns is not as great as the subconscious agony we inflict on ourselves by not reaching our full potential.

Day 33

Flying

[October 14]

Preserved in the rocks of the Dinosaur National Monument are not only the remains of dinosaurs that lived here some 145 million years ago, but also the fossils of sea creatures two or three times older.

My coyote friends began their morning howls at 6:30 A.M. in the sandy hills three hundred yards from me. I could tell from their yelps that there were four or five of them, and I knew their approximate location, but I was never able to see them.

I huffed and puffed south into the wind until I came upon some funky cliff drawings. I learned the red-colored drawings were done by a tribe in about A.D. 1000; it was amazing how well preserved they were in the dry climate and how visible they were from the road.

One of the figures was Kokopelli, the happy, cute, hunch-backed, flute-playing dude. Several miles later I came upon another ancient drawing, a red figure with no neck who was depicted waving both of his hands. He set the tone for a great day.

I climbed 3,000 feet to Colorado's Douglas Pass (8,268 feet) — half of it gradually over thirty-five miles and the last five miles 1,200 feet straight up. I stopped at the top to gaze at the expansive view of mountains and desert

Celebrating the ascent of Douglas Pass with a couple of brews.

and was pleasantly interrupted by a couple of cowboy hunters in a pickup truck. Within a couple of minutes I was fortunate enough to be drinking an icy cold beer with these gentlemen, drawing parallels of my ugly climb to their recent hunting excursion. They had just hauled an elk two miles out of a shallow canyon.

I thoroughly enjoyed a seven-mile descent down the other side of the pass, the headwind ensuring that I didn't scream too fast down the steep drop. I made only average time in the remaining twenty miles to Loma, for the headwind completely destroyed the gradual downhill advantage I had.

The lush irrigated fields of Loma were beautiful against the dusty, sand mountains in the background. I pulled off the road to check out a cool old schoolhouse and had a nice conversation with a couple from Minnesota. The man was born in the area and had spent his childhood there, and he was sharing memories with his wife.

I sprinted five miles east into the little town of Fruita. As I entered a small deli/pizza joint, an old man sitting alone said, "Looks like you need an overload permit."

I grabbed a sandwich and had a great talk with this retired truck driver named Jack Owens. As we ate together, he described how a few days earlier he crashed his bike into a lightpole (the sun temporarily blinded him). He gave me some bike route advice, like only old truckers can, and then told me a stirring account of how a tornado almost took his life on a trip through northern Texas. The twister lifted him and his truck off the highway, turned them sidewise, and then on end. He estimates he was 100 feet in the air at one point. "By an act of God" the tornado set him back down on his wheels and then slammed him into a nearby guardrail. I wasn't sure whether to believe him or not, but as he went on his eyes welled up with tears, and during one point his front dentures came loose during his excited description. So how could he be lying?

I continued on, reaching 100 miles east of Grand Junction, Colorado. I threw my tarp and sleeping bag down in the rolling hills bordering Highway 50, saw two shooting stars, and passed out.

LESSON: Flying downhill on a bike provides one of those moments in life when you feel truly alive. You have just busted your ass on a steep climb, so the descent feels truly deserved. You need to constantly be scanning for upcoming cars or gravel in the road—so you don't eat it at 40 mph—and as a result, your level of awareness is extremely high. Combine this with awesome scenery, wind in your hair, and the fact that you're not pedaling and life is pretty good.

Day 34

The Rolling Eyeball Test
[October 15]

Last night my strategy of putting a couple of fleece jackets under my sleeping bag, rather than wearing them, provided a bit more warmth and protection from the heat-sucking ground.

I began the morning pedaling into a stiff wind from the southwest, and after a couple of hours, I spotted a gravel road which was oriented in a way that gave a magical view of the orange morning sun rising above the sand-colored mountains. Time for a soul-searching session.

I kicked back for four hours—writing in my journal, contemplating the thirty different weather reports I had received from locals regarding the approaching snowstorm, and watching the warm colors of the morning disappear into bright daylight.

The wonderful daytime high temperatures of sixty degrees Fahrenheit were going to soon turn into forty degrees and nighttime lows were to dip to twelve to thirty degrees. The older and crustier the weather reporter was, it seemed, the colder and deeper the snow would supposedly be.

I was partially kicking myself for fly fishing so much in Washington and Idaho, for I probably would have been over the Continental Divide at Monarch Pass two weeks ago if I had concentrated solely on cycling. But the thought of hooking and releasing those browns and rainbows will most likely blunt the pain of frosty toes and fingers at 11,000 feet.

As I stood up from my seated position against a rock, feeling about eighty-five years old, I noticed the headwind had died. Perfect timing. I pedaled up and down the rolling hills that lead to Montrose, covering an enjoyable, sunny forty-nine miles.

LESSON: I can always gauge the severity of an upcoming ride by applying the "Local's Rolling Eyeball Test." When discussing my ride for the day with a permanent resident, I use the following yardstick. If a ride is simply long and relatively flat, the local's eyeballs will only momentarily roll in to the back of his head. If the ride contains several hills that make his 1973 Scout sputter, I will temporarily lose sight of his pupils during the eye roll. If the route for the day is at least ninety miles and contains a mountain pass with a climb of 2,000 feet, his face will cringe, transparently revealing his thought pattern that "this guy needs to get a job." His eyeballs then roll completely into the back of his skull for two seconds as he simultaneously throws back his head.

Day 35

Of Eagles and Buzzards

[October 16]

Based on the warnings of the locals, I envisioned a day of icy roads and deep snow. I thought I'd be pushing my bloated bicycle up passes through six inches of snow and skating down steep descents.

Instead I enjoyed virtually ideal conditions. The sky was cloudless, the temperature reached forty degrees (ideal for the day's steep climbs), the roads were relatively dry, and a wonderful tailwind helped scoot me along.

I climbed 2,100 feet to Cerro Summit and received the now familiar "What's-that-fool-doing-with-a-bike-up-here?" look from a dozen or so people in vehicles. The sweet tailwind and my fresh legs made the climb nearly effortless. I ripped off my fleece shirt for a few minutes to let the cold air dry my clammy body, then I added three fleece shirts and a windbreaker and be-

The GuNNisON River BasiN drains close to 4,000 square miles of trout couNtry, including huNdreds of small streams.

79

Blue Mesa
Reservoir is the
largest body of
water in Colorado
and provides
year-round
fishing.

gan a sunny, scenic 800-foot descent into the little village of Cimarron.

I stopped at Newberry's General Store, more to check out the old soulful little place than to buy anything. I began reading the newspaper articles from the 1970s on display there that highlighted two crazy young rock climbers scaling different routes in Gunnison Canyon. I saw an older version of the young, longhaired daredevil from the papers in the store drinking coffee. His name was Jim Newberry and he began telling a few stories of his climbing glory days, adding that he hadn't climbed in ten years because he "lost his nerve."

He said that in the early stages of some of their difficult climbs they would gaze into the sky at the natural beauty that surrounded them. If they spotted a soaring eagle riding the convection currents above them, they confidently continued their climb, and if instead they viewed a soaring buzzard, they abruptly ended it.

I finished another tailwind-aided 1,600-foot climb to Blue Mesa Summit and hauled downhill, mesmerized by the whitecaps on the Blue Mesa Reservoir below. I followed the shores of the reservoir until the lake slowly reverted into the Gunnison River.

The subtle downhill ride into Gunnison Canyon combined with the strong tailwind and spectacular Gunnison Canyon scenery to make the day's ride a memorable

A grub break overlooking Blue Mesa Reservoir on the way to Gunnison, Colorado.

one. The day was so ideal that I finished it by staying the night at a hotel. I experienced life's sweet contrast again as I slipped into the hotel's Jacuzzi, remembering the rock-hard, cold, sandy ground of the last few nights. Great day.

LeSSON: Live life with your mind and eyes open so that you can sense the eagles of life that lead us to new heights and the buzzards of life that warn us against moving down less favorable paths.

Day 36

ChaiNs Required
[October 17]

The Colorado State Patrol's road conditions phone line stated that my final climb over the Continental Divide and Monarch Pass was "snow packed and icy; chains are required for all commercial vehicles and recommended for all others."

I'm dumb but not stupid. The 4,000-foot climb and descent with my skinny little road bike tires would be entertaining, but not intelligent. I spent the day tooling around Gunnison and performing maintenance on my bicycle. I laughed to myself as I came across dozens of Western State College of Colorado students moving lethargically downtown with a glaze over their bloodshot eyes from a lively Saturday night.

I talked with a dozen or so friendly locals — the most memorable being a crazed forty-year-old ex-cyclist and his sixty-eight-year-old girlfriend. My abs ached from laughing at his hilarious stories of his 1,200-mile bike trip fifteen years ago.

I was going to cross the Continental Divide tomorrow even if I had to push my bike half the way. It will mark the beginning of the end of the beautiful mountain scenery, trout streams, and straight uphill climbs.

LESSON: You cannot undertake a trip of this nature without developing a unique bond to your only true, faithful companion of the journey…your bicycle. And you cannot travel 4,000 miles, sharing laughs and tears with this true companion, without developing a multitude of nicknames for it. My Trek 520 is also affectionately known as: Pack Mule, Harley Hog, Wind Plow, The Stinking Headwind Magnet, Old Diamond Saddle, and More Spokes than Brains.

Day 37

Up aNd Over the Divide
[October 18]

I left Gunnison like a caged dog. It would be a relief to get over the final pass, knowing the remainder of my trip should be relatively flat and snow-free.

It would also be slightly satisfying to complete my mountainous, late-fall route after at least one hundred people before and during my ride called it foolish and recommended that I re-route.

Fifteen miles out of Gunnison, a white Subaru slipped behind me and began honking. My buddy Matt's wonderfully nice girlfriend, Nikol, then began commenting on my lack of perceptiveness, as she had honked several times before I acknowledged. It was great seeing a familiar, friendly face. We high-fived and made dinner plans for my arrival in Salida.

The terrain rose gradually 800-feet over the first thirty-five miles of the day until I reached Monarch Pass. In eight miles the beast gained 3,000 feet. I was a bit nostalgic climbing the summit; I knew the challenge in the next 2,000 miles would be a flat perseverance test rather than intense, physical climbs of the mountain country.

The climb was relatively easy, the only challenge being the thinner air at 11,000 feet. I was certainly very pleased that I had smoked that raunchy cigar with my brother during our fishing trip last week.

At the exact moment I reached the summit, the sky filled with huge snowflakes. With my heat-generating climb over, I scrambled to put on every piece of clothing I owned. The twenty-mile descent into a slight headwind was more numbing than exhilarating, but I welcomed it. As the poetic Department of Transportation worker said at the summit, as she compared climbs to descents, "I hope you enjoy your ride down. It seems like it would be more tolerable to freeze your ass off than work your ass off."

I rallied down the mountain as fast as I could, stopping three times not only to warm against the wind chill but also to catch my breath. As I pedaled hard into Salida, an unfamiliar white pickup truck pulled off onto the shoulder blocking my path. My buddy Ray, who I hadn't seen in two years, got out of the truck and snorted, "I knew it had to be you Red. No one else is stupid enough to be riding today!"

I was amazed to find that I could barely form words. The cold descent somehow affected my jaw and tongue, causing me to slur every other word. I laughed as we exchanged fishing and travel stories.

I enjoyed a great dinner with Nikol. The simple pleasures of warmth, food, and conversation seemed amplified by the chilly ride of a couple hours ago. I had just met Nikol a week ago, so at dinner I conducted an extensive interview, background check, and psychiatric test to ensure she was suitable for my best buddy. She passed.

I slept the night on her living room floor, picking up approximately three pounds of dog hair on my fleece pullover. I'm hoping this addition adds to the insulation properties of the garment.

LESSON: You realize you are becoming desperate on a steep bicycle climb when one or more of these three things occur:

1. You repeatedly attempt to put your bike into granny gear, even though it has been in this lowest gear for a full hour. (This is very similar and related to repeatedly opening the same empty refrigerator door, hoping that a new morsel of food has appeared.)

2. You work extremely hard to keep your tires on the white shoulder stripe because this painted line fills the porous asphalt surface of the road, allows less friction between your tires and the street, and provides a very, very slight increase in velocity.

3. You wholeheartedly welcome huge semi trucks that pass within six inches and draw you into a sort of air suction field that propels you two to three feet uphill.

Day 38

Riding the Edge
[October 19]

There was two inches of snow outside this morning, and I was pretty charged up to be over the Continental Divide. Weather reports and road conditions were now removed from my short list of concerns on this trip, so all that remained was locating wide enough road shoulders and finding my next Pop-Tart.

I thanked my gracious host Nikol and headed seven miles east to Matt's fly shop to take care of a few administrative items. As I rode along the Arkansas River in Big Sheep Canyon, I was amazed at how beautiful the mountain views were and how quickly the snow disappeared.

I spent the day maintaining my bike, writing journal entries, and talking with one of Matt's fly fishing guides, Ezra, a formally trained chef turned river guide. Definitely an interesting dude to talk with. Ezra had spent a portion of his childhood in Europe, where he developed a fascination with sleek, motorized model planes after seeing some old men in a park using them. As we talked, he tinkered with one of the planes and described the laborious hours required to sculpt and construct one. Since the guiding season was over, he was also using this time to sort out his next destination.

A snowy morning on the Arkansas River.

I left my fly rod, waders, and boots at the fly shop for Matty to mail home to me. Although I'd certainly enjoy a more streamlined profile without this gear, I doubt that it was an adequate trade-off for the joy it brought me.

I headed out at 4:30 P.M., following the hairpin curves along the Arkansas River. I drooled as I passed sections of the river I had fished over the years... and was reminded that the fly fishing part of the trip was over.

At dusk I scanned the rocky shore for bighorn sheep as I rode, but the nonexistent road shoulder and passing semitrailer trucks distracted me slightly. As darkness approached, I thought it would be better to cut my ride a bit short and freeze tonight in the canyon rather than pedal a couple of more hours and risk being smeared onto the grill of one of the passing trucks.

I spent a quiet night along the river at an empty campground, imagining what a great place it must be in the middle of the summer when the river is jammed with happy whitewater rafters. A sharp contrast to this cold, quiet evening.

LESSON: Many of the roads I've traveled have been characterized by low traffic counts and very narrow shoulders. Every once in a while my front tire barely skirted a four-inch drop-off on the right side. That drop-off mostly contained soft sand, rocks, or boulders; all things I would like to avoid.

Almost invariably I noticed that in those herky-jerky times—when my lack of balance could have dumped me into the rocks—if I stared and focused on the road, I ended up on the road. And during those moments I freaked out and was concentrating on the ugly rocks and gravel to the right, I somehow found my front tire moving there.

In life we need to condition ourselves to consciously focus on where we want to go, what we want to happen, and who we want to meet rather than their negative counterparts. What our minds focus on is where we subconsciously steer.

Flower Ladies

[October 20]

A long, spiky frost covered my bivy sack from head to toe. I could tell it was going to be one of those character-building mornings.

I moved quickly, following the slight downhill through the cold canyon and enjoying only the fact that there was not much traffic early in the morning. The sun had yet to reach within the canyon walls and my cold feet were like stumps at the end of my legs. But I knew I had only seven or eight miles before I reached more open terrain and sweet sunshine.

I heartily welcomed the 700-foot climb into Parkdale near the Royal Gorge; it allowed me to work some blood through my frosty extremities and also marked the end of the cold canyon. I eventually coasted through a six-mile, 1,000-foot descent into Canon City, another one of those low-output, high-enjoyment moments.

Julia had requested earlier that I visit the grave of her great-great-grandfather Charles Linneer, who had been a respected tailor in Canon City in the 1860s. So I pulled off on the first side street and came across a cool floral shop. I began explaining my situation in hopes of finding instructions to the cemetery when the double-trouble duo of Ilene and Arlene took me under their wings.

Since they specialize in memorial services and Memorial Day gifts, they had all the connections for finding the exact plot where this old chap was put to rest. They were delightful ladies. I hauled up the hill

Grave marker of Julia's great-great-grandfather Charles Linneer. Canon City, CO

to the dusty graveyard and found the old beat-up marker for Charles. I weeded his plot, rearranged a few of the silk flowers, and made an imprint for Julia using crayons and waxpaper, courtesy of the flower ladies. The cemetery's beautiful mountain backdrop more than made up for the dry soil and burnt grass.

I stopped in at Wendy's, using my free coupons from the dudes in Blackfoot, Idaho, and proceeded to spread my sleeping bag, bivy, and the rest of my gear out along Main Street in order to allow the heavy frost to dry. I received more than a few stares as I jammed my face with food, surrounded by all my worldly possessions, completely unconcerned.

Virtually my entire seventy-eight-mile ride today was into a pesky headwind that pretty much neutralized the elevation decrease. I rode until dark, working my way through the smells of Mexican food and burnt brush near Pueblo. I finally found a somewhat grassy playground, gazed at the stars, and hit the rack.

Lesson: It seems the older we get, the less we care about social acceptance, whether it's as minor as frying your underwear on Main Street under a horde of stares or pursuing a lifestyle or higher principle that gives you peace of mind, while possibly chafing others.

The Royal Gorge on the Arkansas River is some 10 miles long and more than 1,000 feet deep. The Royal Gorge Suspension Bridge, built in 1929, spans the canyon.

Day 40

206 Miles in 21 Hours
[October 21]

The mountain passes of the West provided solid physical challenge and an enjoyable time. I had to get stoked up in order to climb 3,000 feet in four miles and face the possibility of snow and funky weather conditions. But after reaching the summits, I was rewarded with high-speed restful descents, in addition to fantastic, hard-earned views.

The flat prairie land of eastern Colorado didn't provide for that. In the West, the diversity of the views and the burning in my legs during climbs also masked the soreness in my back, neck, butt, and hands. After only one day in the flatlands, I needed a little charge.

AN eNdless ribboN of couNtry road headiNg iNto the plaiNs.

I had set my alarm for one-thirty in the morning and began pedaling in the dark by two. I wanted to see how far I could pedal my bloated pack mule in a day. It was just a tad bit nippy in the morning, the thermometer read twenty-nine degrees, but the wind chill, due to my velocity, made it much colder.

I rode along the dark, traffic-free streets in a twilight-zone-like trance. After three hours, I found an open convenience store and happily indulged in a cup of hot chocolate. It was amazing how the average and slightly boring conversation I initiated with the cashier extended well past its useful life of three minutes to thirty minutes, as I subconsciously extended my stop in order to raise my body temperature in the warm, bright store. That same hour I lost my beautiful, almost-full moon as it sank below the horizon and turned the night opaque.

I passed through the sleeping Colorado towns of Fowler, Manzanola, and Rocky Ford too focused and cold to pay much attention to their features. I knew these first few hours and the weary last few would be the most difficult so I just pedaled hard, waiting for the sun to rise.

I enjoyed a manly breakfast in La Junta and was

able to shed most of my bulky clothes. I sucked in the warmth of the sun near Las Animas and was treated to a show by the white-breasted hawks that patrolled Highway 50. I watched as one glided off a telephone pole, hovered over the brush, made a quick stab for a mouse...and missed. It seemed as though a beautiful hawk was perched on one of every ten telephone poles.

I hit 100 miles before 11:30 A.M., but yesterday's stubborn headwind returned and began to impede my progress. By 1 P.M. I had consumed an ungodly amount of food, including five pieces of fruit, five Pop-Tarts, a full box of Muesli cereal, four scrambled eggs, two huge pancakes, four granola bars, a monster twelve-inch turkey and veggie hoagie, German chocolate cake, two cold cans of Beefaroni, eight bottles of Gatorade, and two peanut butter sandwiches.

I entered Holly, Colorado, and was treated to a canopy of mature trees over the main street. It was exciting watching the terrain change so quickly from the wintry mountain passes I'd been in a couple of days ago. I pedaled in the dark into Kansas, the full moon illuminating the pastures in front of me. Dark bushes across the prairies appeared in the moonlight like grazing buffalo, allowing me to imagine what the region looked like before the white man's slaughter.

Just as I was growing tired in the dark, a magical moment occurred. There were no vehicles on the road and my rhythmic pedaling was about to hypnotize me when three figures excitedly pranced alongside me on the road. Three beautiful horses galloped along a fence beside me for half a mile, all spunky and perky in the moonlight. It was almost unreal as they looked directly at me, modified their speed to my pace, and happily raced me along the fence.

The ride began to get challenging as the terrain turned into a series of 100-foot climbs and descents. At the same time, fatigue was truly setting in and the swirling headwind began to pick up even more. I finally hit the 200-mile mark and began a laborious

6-mile effort to find a suitable place to crash. I settled on a dirt field that smelled like fresh manure, but so did I, so what the hell. I covered 206 miles today in twenty-one hours of pedaling, fifty of them into an ornery headwind.

Lesson: I believe we are put on the planet to find out what we can do with what God gave us—brains, muscle, creativity. Making the decision to do less than you can do is a slap in the face of the grantor of these gifts.

Day 41

Finding a Natural Flow in Kansas

[October 22]

I set a record last night and only rolled over twice in my sleep instead of the usual forty times. Exhaustion will do that.

The sky was bright and the air warm, but as I stepped out of my sleeping bag, a blast of cold air hit me. I had forgotten that last night, even in my delirious state, I had found a utility pole and group of thick bushes to break the wind.

As I geared up to ride, I remember commenting to myself how beautifully clear the sky was today. In the time it took me to dress, the sky filled with a thick, grayish black sheet of smoke. Five miles away a farmer was burning his field, spewing smoke

Clear skies turn green during a field burn-off near Garden City, Kansas.

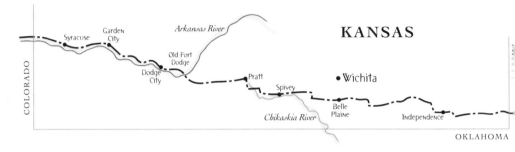

across the entire landscape and turning the sun's brightness into an ugly, pale haze.

I realize burning fields nourishes the soil, kills diseases, and was probably practiced by his great-great-grandfather. But I cannot think of a more selfish act than reconditioning your field forty acres at a time while forcing 30,000 people in a nearby town to suck your smoke while you literally block the sun's rays.

After ten miles I stopped at a small café for breakfast and met an interesting Native American guy my age with a long pigtail. He caught me shaving in the restaurant bathroom, began laughing, and asked what I was up to. I told him of my ride and of the Conservation Resource Alliance's work as we headed to the salad bar, and as we parted he told me "do not work too hard pedaling your bike, move with the natural flow."

I headed toward Dodge City for my rendezvous with Julia this weekend, hoping to utilize some of the backroads we had found on our topo maps. But as I reached my turnoff, I found these nice, thick, red-lined roads to be gravel and dusty.

At a small gas station in the middle of nowhere, I met Todd, who was driving a UPS truck. United Parcel Service must have a "nice-guy screening test" or "nice-guy training program" because virtually every UPS driver I've met in my life has been a quality individual. We talked of the hidden beauty of Kansas and his plans for retirement. We wished each other well, but connected again thirty miles down the road at a convenience store. This time he told me to spoil myself and stay at a quaint bed-and-breakfast that he knew of in Dodge City, and so I did.

I met Julia there and enjoyed the contrast between solitude, twenty-one-hour bike rides, and manure fields and wonderful companionship and homey accommodations.

LESSON: Do not work too hard, move with the natural flow.

Day 42

Signs of Other Travelers
[October 23]

Our bed-and-breakfast overlooked Boot Hill, the location where lowlifes, gunslingers, and just bad-luck victims were buried by the sheriff during Dodge City's wild and wooly frontier days. Most of the dwellers in that plot of land were buried with their boots on or had them used for a pillow.

We walked through Boot Hill Museum, gazing at the collection of old guns, equipment, and clothing from Dodge City's heyday. But we left with a large, empty feeling after learning more about the slaughter of the north and south herds of buffalo...numbers that ran in the millions. Each hunter killed hundreds of buffalo a day, letting the corpses rot on the plains. If all the buffalo were destroyed, the strategy went, the plains Indian's way of life would be destroyed, and the white man's progress could continue unabated. It took the hunters only four to five years to eradicate the buffalo.

We stopped at a cozy, authentic Mexican restaurant and ate our fair share of tacos. We then shot out of town to the west in search of a portion of the Santa Fe Trail that was said to still contain ruts from wagon wheels that rode along it over a century ago. We were fired up to discover the wagon trails of our ancestors, feel the pain of their journey, and taste a little Americana, but instead we met a shaggy, toothless dog and its owners, Jeff and Lisa from Rolla, Missouri. We had a wonderful time talking with them, and since

Attempting to find the Santa Fe Trail with Jeff, Lisa, and their toothless dog near Dodge City, Kansas.

Jeff was a professor of geological engineering and he didn't locate the famous tracks either, we didn't feel quite as inadequate.

We capped off a fine, relaxing day with a local high-school football game, watching the Dodge City boys get lambasted 56-0 by halftime. The halftime show of 50 three- to six-year-old girls performing a pom-pom cheerleading routine filled the stadium with cuteness. It, of course, prompted Julia's patented speech on how young girls should be participating in sports themselves and striving for excellence in other disciplines rather than wasting their time cheering for boys.

LESSON: Sometimes white man no good.

Complexities of Homelessness

[October 24]

Julia left early to begin her sixteen-hour trek home, and I spent the morning chatting with our B & B owners Jacques and Louisa, discovering the weird winding road that led them from Montreal to California to Dodge City.

I loved their story of how they truly disliked each other when they first met. She thought Jacques was arrogant and self-absorbed, while he thought Louisa was a freaky girl with braces and a disgusting habit of removing those little rubberbands in her mouth before eating at parties.

I grabbed a bite to eat on the way out of town. While I inhaled a couple of grilled chicken sandwiches, the local bike-shop owner walked into the restaurant and scoured the place looking for the yahoo with the overloaded bike. We traded touring stories and he graciously offered to open his closed shop to replace my 2,300-mile-old balding rear tire. I told him thanks but that I was antsy to get the hell out of Dodge.

On my way out of town, I came across a sight that we've all probably seen…a crusty old man with a sign that read, "Homeless. I have no money, no food."

I've always wondered about the background of these individuals and what makes them tick, or not tick. I kicked back and talked with Tom for forty minutes. We bonded quickly since I could totally relate to the hobo lifestyle of sleeping in funky places under the stars. We traded stories of freezing our butts off at night and I found him to be a pretty coherent guy, definitely not mentally handicapped.

Of the 1,203 miles of the Santa Fe Trail between Old Franklin, Missouri, and Santa Fe, New Mexico, more than 200 miles of ruts and trace remain visible; some 30 miles of these are protected on federal lands.

He spoke of just recently getting beat up by four teenagers in Manhattan, Kansas, and how a good Samaritan found him freezing one night under a picnic table and ended up buying him new clothes, a coat, and a backpack totaling $508.

I have always believed that anyone of able mind and body who chooses to live on handouts from the state rather than work hard and contribute to society simply needs a swift kick in the pants. This seems especially true in an economic environment that has been so healthy over the last seven to eight years, where many businesses will do whatever it takes to keep hardworking employees happy.

But every issue is more complex than it appears on the surface. Tom was definitely not of weak character. He was a survivor who braved freezing cold nights and scraped and clawed to feed himself each day. But for every scenario I gave him to live a different lifestyle, to secure a steady job, and find a cheap place to live, he supplied seven excuses why it wouldn't work.

Yet I found most of his excuses were external in nature; they painted him as a victim of every environmental factor known to man. He had completely lost his personal power. His life was a contradiction—he could tough out harsh daily living conditions but could not deal with the pain and discipline of living a structured life. He both loved and hated the way he lived. He smugly enjoyed receiving handouts, not working hard, not having a disciplined routine, not having a boss, not paying taxes, but hated not having enough to eat, not being warm, and not having control.

I worked hard not to let my jaw hit the ground when the skinny, scruffy, deep-wrinkled, eighty-three-year-old-looking man told me he was fifty-three.

I rode to Old Fort Dodge, attempting to analyze my conversation with Tom and figure his whole program out. I decided that I wasn't going to ever completely understand and that I didn't need to as long as

I had a deeper empathy for where he stood. Some things just are.

I sat back in a grassy park in Old Fort Dodge and wrote in my journal for four hours. George Armstrong Custer, Philip Henry Sheridan, and "Wild Bill" Hickok all had their time at this fort, which was built to protect travelers along the Santa Fe Trail from Indian raids. It now served as a Kansas soldiers home, and I watched the old men in wheelchairs at their windows as they watched me.

Man, I've got to keep living, to keep taking on challenges, to continue to grab the fun from each day, so when I trade places with the old man in the wheelchair with the broken-down body, I can remember the wonderful days I was blessed with, not regretting the things I never tried. At the very least, I'm working on the broken-down-body part with this trip.

A resident of the home came out on the porch just as I was packing up to leave. As I decided to go over and talk with him, a parade of children in colorful Halloween costumes and armed with boxes of treats paraded across the park, past the man, and into the residence area. It was a touching moment as I watched the old man's blank face light up as he wished every single passing child a happy Halloween. I observed for a while from a distance and then took off.

I rode a total of only twenty miles to the tiny town of Ford, headed down a dirt side road, and found a wheat field with a row of trees properly oriented to block the wind. The wind, of course, changed directions in the middle of the night, but it was still a cozy cubbyhole.

LESSON: Some things just are.

The Lost Boy

[October 25]

After a quick peanut-butter-and-jelly breakfast, I began pedaling into the sunshine. Five miles into the day
I came upon a scruffy cyclist on a beat-up bike; he
appeared to be touring, but maybe not. Instead of panniers, he wore a backpack that to me had "sore ass"
written all over it. His bike was pretty soulful, with
chipped paint and a big grandma-style seat.

He never saw me approaching since he was off his
bike working intently on his brakes, so as I passed I
yelled, "How's it going?"

"Terrible," he replied. I turned around and got to
know "The Lost Boy." His name was Doug. His wife
had grabbed their son and left him, and he had just
biked from California to Florida hoping to find roof-
ing work as a result of hurricane Irene. Now he was
returning to California.

He didn't have tools to fix his brakes. He didn't
know why his wife left him. He didn't know why he
was heading back to California. He didn't know where
to cross the Continental Divide. He didn't know if he
should just stop along the way and find a job. And he
didn't know where his next meal was coming from.

I helped him fix his brakes with my Allen
wrenches, gave him the last of my peanut butter and
jelly, and delivered a Knute Rockne pep talk. After an
hour or so he said, "Thanks man. My brakes are fixed
and my attitude's changed." We shook hands and
looked at each other with the same "yeah, I know your
ass and legs hurt, but in life you've got to keep pedaling" look and headed our separate ways.

I rode starving into the town of Mullinville and
walked into a ten-table roadside café. It was one of

those places where if someone asks you a question, you reply to the entire restaurant. I ended up having lunch with an old trucker named John who sported a white Santa-Claus-style beard and about ten spots where skin cancer had been burned off his nose. He talked of being on the road for twenty-seven years, close calls on truck crashes, and his plans for retirement. I sat amazed as he chugged cup after cup of coffee.

I rode on across the Kansas plains, which lacked much diversity but were beautiful still. Freshly sprouted winter wheat extended for miles and red-tailed hawks soared in the sky.

I arrived in the well-kept town of Pratt hoping to find an ATM machine. In a well-kept bank parking lot I asked a well-kept professional lady where the nearest cash machine was, and she replied, "Right behind you." She then proceeded for about twenty minutes to ask me every detail of my life. Like virtually all the Kansans I'd met, she was unbelievably friendly and had a story of another cyclist she'd met that attempted a similar ride.

I headed to a gas station/convenience store and had a colorful thirty-minute conversation with Bernie, the mechanic. He was a great guy and explained how his interest in bicycles blossomed when he received his second DUI and lost his license for a year. I then rode to a nearby park and wrote in my journal until dusk, allowing the moderate headwind to subside.

I headed south a couple hours later with virtually no wind and enjoyed a monster sunset over the endless wheat fields. The orange sky lingered for an hour. As I began to head east again, the orange sun gave way to a rising orange moon, which I stared at for two hours.

My calm ride came to a screeching halt as I came within two feet of running over a medium-sized animal directly in my path. As it scurried off onto the shoulder, I circled, grabbed my flashlight, and found a skunk with its tail straight up, scratching the grass and making a strange skunk sound. I prayed my bike's radius was tight enough to stay out of the spray range, and it was. I finished my 100 miles that day and slept in deep grass bordering a wheat field.

Lesson: Yeah, I know your ass and legs hurt, but in life you've got to keep pedaling.

Day 45

Solid
[October 26]

Mornings are now a balmy forty-five degrees and life is good. I made good time hauling across the plains before the wind decided to stir. A funky mist covered the wheat fields in low-lying areas.

I stopped in the small town of Spivey at 9 A.M., and as I got off my bike at the post office, a friendly farmer struck up a conversation describing how much he enjoys riding his bicycle after his tasks for the day are complete. I politely let him in line ahead of me, but the lady postmaster quickly popped up, "Don't mind him. He's just after a free cup of coffee."

"I know her," he replied. "We're shacking up together."

I spent the next hour talking with this retired wheat farmer and his postmaster wife of forty years about everything from his four-acre bass pond to the state of America's work ethic. The people of Kansas have to be the friendliest and most down-to-earth people in the country. As I mounted my trusty bike, the farmer named Dee Brown said, "Jeff, a few years ago I would have asked to ride with you a couple days."

"Damn, that would be cool," I thought.

I continued east, enjoying a scenic view of the shallow Chikaskia River. I battled a variable wind that blew from the south most of the time, but switched every ten minutes to howl directly in my face. I stopped in Conway Springs to make a couple of phone calls when a sporty-looking cyclist on a fancy Italian racing bike pulled up and gave me the quick "cyclist lookover" to see what I was all about.

My blue-collar biking mentality usually categorizes these fancy pants cyclists with the sporty jerseys and slick glasses as more full of themselves than having much biking ability or grit. But as I shared the road for eight miles with Caroline, I found a tough, competent cycling freak who is the state's top-ranked mountain biker in her class.

Her true nature surfaced when one of her thin racing tires temporarily lodged itself at a railroad crossing, sending her sprawling at 16 mph across the pavement. She was up and riding within three seconds, more concerned with the functioning of her bike than the several layers of leg and arm epidermal tissue she left on the road. I then learned this thirty-year-old-looking lady was fifty-three— the same age as Tom, my homeless buddy from Dodge City.

Along my ride I passed the Ninnescah River and was fortunate to overcome the sweating and nausea associated with fly fishing withdrawal. I crossed a bridge and spotted three largemouth bass holding in a small run, while a nice three-pounder worked the surface, rising every five seconds.

Fine dining in the Kansas countryside.

I pedaled until I reached Belle Plaine, the closest point I would come to Wichita, Kansas's largest city.

We had a couple of promotional TV interviews set up there, so I cut my ride short. I scouted around town and found a series of softball fields that would be ideal for sleeping quarters and, more important, found a hose to shower with.

I dined at Happy's Restaurant, more attracted to its name than its appearance. Virtually all the tables said grace before beginning their meal, and the enjoyable waitresses made me give them a personalized tour of my hot-rod bicycle.

I covered sixty-five easy, flat miles today, once again working the jaw muscles a bit harder than the legs. I thoroughly enjoyed the warm night, tall grass, and open sky at my softball field campground.

The Kansa, a native North American tribe, originally lived along the lower Kansas River. The word Kansas means "people of the south wind."

LESSON: Kansas people are solid.

Day 46

100 Miles
[October 27]

The Wichita TV boys blew us off and, unfortunately, I wasn't able to start pedaling until noon, which put a small kink in my plans for a 100-mile day.

I continued pedaling south and east across the prairies, the southern legs facing into the teeth of a stop-sign-shaking 30-mph headwind. My scientific study found that six out of ten Kansas people in passing cars waved to the anemic-looking man on the overloaded bike. Along my route, I passed dozens of homey, grandmas-on-the-front-porch, apple-pies-in-the-oven white farmhouses.

I met an engaging farmer originally from Battle Creek, Michigan, a mountain biker who rides along cow paths in the surrounding fields (always "trying to miss the soft, sticky bumps"), a politician wannabe in Moline who gets easily fired up discussing campaign reform, and dozens of old men in bib overalls who all smiled and laughed when I told them I was pedaling 4,000 miles.

I sucked it up and finished my 100-miler at 11 P.M., following the peaceful, empty backcountry roads.

LESSON: In bicycle touring, you can focus your attention solely on the two feet ahead of your front tire, ensuring that you miss pot-holes and glass, but also wonderful scenery and directional signs. You may also gaze far ahead, absorbing mountain views and sunsets as well as nails, tacks, and thorns.

One of the keys of life is riding the fine line between the macro view of your life—and experiencing the gifts around you—while being detailed enough to handle the short-term demons of daily living that mark a successful career and family life.

Day 47

Still Crazy
[October 28]

I actually woke up in the middle of last night sweating and was forced to rip off a couple of layers. Life is getting easy.

I felt fresh in the morning, even after my late ride last night, and I was fired up to pound out another flat 100-miler. I rode five miles into Independence, Kansas, so hungry that I could feel my body digesting itself.

I stopped at the Cowboy Café because its exterior looked like it had some character and the parking lot was quite full. As I settled into the large restaurant and absorbed the ambiance, it appeared to me that the clientele here was in some sort of race to see who could kill themselves the fastest. The people at every table were chain smoking and, unfortunately, appeared to have had a few too many of the café's Bubba Burgers over the years.

My mother-figure waitress, Trude, and I bonded right away. She told me how the last two men in her life abused her and that she hadn't been on a date in three and one-half years. I told her that George Washington had once said, "It is better to be alone than in the presence of poor company." To which she said "Amen" and passed her address on to me so that I could mail her a postcard from Savannah to verify I survived the trip.

My rear tire was now completely bald after 2,500 miles of abuse, so I slowly pedaled down Main Street and noticed the colorful decorations of Independence's 58th Annual Neewollah Festival as I headed toward the bike shop. Street vendors were everywhere and the people seemed entirely too festive for Thursday at nine-thirty in the morning.

Owner Mike Thompson completely fixed me up with a first-class tune-up, dropping everything to accommodate me. As I waited for a couple of hours, I made a dozen business calls and had a dozen people say, "I see you're in town for the Neewollah Festival." I thought to myself, "Festival. Man, I'm on a bike ride. I'm on a schedule. I'm on the program."

As darkness rolled in at around seven, I was glad I still hadn't left Independence and by then had figured out that Neewollah was Halloween spelled backwards.

I don't think I've ever met as many unique people in such a narrow window of time. They were all classics: a mural painter who offered to make a similar ride with me next year (not if I want my present job); Paul, an old World War II fighter pilot who flew 387 missions in the South Pacific; a mountain of a man named Dellon who works with antique tractors and tried to lure me to his personal five-acre pond for a bass tourney; a funky red-haired lady who had her bull dog puppy dressed in a Dallas Cowboy jersey; and Ken, a quality guy and a long-distance runner with an electrical engineering degree who was very active in his son's Boy Scout troop.

Ken gave me the local play-by-play call as we watched the hilarious Doo Dah Parade, an event dedicated to letting adult Kansans dress up in costumes that concealed their identities and allowed them to get as wacky as possible. I appropriately spent the evening on the grounds of a home for the mentally disabled, flicking spiders off my tarp as I wrote in my journal by flashlight.

The Neewollah Festival in full swing.

LESSON: Schedule Smedule.

The Country's Friendliest People

[October 29]

Completely blowing off yesterday's ride in favor of Neewollah buffoonery obviously angered the cycle gods.

I awoke early in the morning to a strong 35-mph crosswind that was easily gusting to 45–50 mph. Ten miles into my ride I found my rear tire flat due to a tiny thorn. Five miles later a small metal sliver again flattened my rear tire. I then discovered my only spare tube had a Schraeder valve rather than the Presta valve that I required, so it was worthless.

Performing mechanical wizardry outside Independence, Kansas.

I had also been tapping into my food reserves over the last few days in order to consume some of the older, nastier stuff, so I was now completely out of food. It was noon and I'd only eaten a less-than-tasty can of green beans. The crosswind also was a fine challenge. It was almost like making the longest right-hand turn in history since nearly a quarter of my weight was leaning constantly into the wind to balance my bike.

But as always, things turn around fast. I came to a town named Altamont that was not on my map, and it contained a great little grocery store. I gazed down Main Street and witnessed a nonstop tunnel of dust blasting through the canyon created by the town's buildings. I did the "overshop because you're starving" thing, found a grassy spot between the post office and the grocery store that was out of the wind, and happily grubbed.

I was a pretty interesting sight, though I didn't realize it. The strong crosswind that had been kicking up dust from the farmers' fields had applied ninety layers of caked dirt over my face and neck. Two old ladies passed by, and we enjoyed a pleasant conversation until I made a fatal mistake committed only by non-Kansans. On my long rides I loved watching the hawks ride the convection currents above me and then swoop down to scoop up a field mouse or other varmint. The old ladies informed me that they were chicken hawks or red-tailed hawks. Being a college basketball fan, I then followed up by asking them, "What then is a Kansas Jayhawk?"

The once polite, conservative, and gentle ladies looked at each other and then pitifully at me and laughed a hardy Kansan laugh. I gathered that a Jayhawk is not a bird, but instead is a nickname for a Kansan. At that moment, I went from being just ugly and poor to ugly, poor, and stupid. Our conversation soon ended and I thought, "Wow, I guess I know what the lesson of the day is."

I then talked with a friendly chap who had positioned himself near the post office to collect donations for the Lions Club. Fifteen minutes into our conversation, one of the old ladies returned and thrust three dollars into my hand. I laughed and said, "No, no, no, no, no. I appreciate it, but don't need it...no, no, no."

The sweet lady turned away briskly saying, "You buy yourself some warm dinner tonight." She walked quickly away, having made her contribution to the betterment of the ugly, poor, and stupid of the world.

I needed to fax a document, so I headed to the only professional-looking building in town — the Farm Bureau Insurance office. As they graciously agreed to help me, I had fun talking with the agents in the of-

The term "Jayhawker" was used at the beginning of the American Civil War to refer to bands of antislavery guerrillas and irregular troops along the Kansas-Missouri border.

fice, learning of the huge number of crop damage claims they were processing due to the four-month drought. I made the mistake of mentioning my recent Jayhawk story and became the target of more abuse. When they refused to charge me for my thirteen-page fax, I happily transferred my three-dollar gift to them.

As I left Altamont, a police car quickly maneuvered across the road, blocking both lanes of traffic. As I rode the half-mile up to the vehicle, I noticed the cop striking a macho posture in front of his cruiser with its lights flashing.

I thought, "Man, there must have been a robbery; this is the only road in and out of town and the cop looks serious." I laughed as a string of forty kindergartners in bright Halloween costumes happily crossed the road looking at all the traffic stopped for them. Small towns are cool.

I pedaled hard toward dusk, finally nearing the Kansas-Missouri border. Many informed me that Kansas would be a true drag, the worst part of my ride. To me Kansas was cornfields, white farmhouses, soaring hawks, perfect rows of young winter wheat, small-town water towers visible from six miles away, armadillo road kills, stinky cattle feed lots that extended for miles, unstoppable wind, Neewollah, and the friendliest people in the country.

At around 5 P.M. I reached Missouri's welcome sign and observed the landscape change from flat fields to rolling, oak-filled hills. As I pleasantly hauled along Missouri Highway 96, its narrow shoulder disappeared, coinciding exactly with the coming of darkness. I had no business riding at night on this road but was damn close to finishing my 100-miler. I bravely and stupidly flashed my puny Maglite as each truck approached, prayed each driver had impeccable vision, and pumped my legs at a sprinter's pace. Just as I reached mile 100, a pissed trucker blasted his horn, laying on it for about ten seconds as he passed me.

Enough of this nonsense. I pulled down a quiet,

safe dirt road, pedaled a mile or two, found the only pasture without a fence, and set up my tarp to prepare for the potentially stormy night.

As I settled in, a passing pickup truck spotted my bike, hit his brakes, and threw his vehicle into reverse. Hmmm. As he clicked his bright lights on me from fifty feet away, I felt a bit vulnerable. Actually, I felt like I was standing naked on a stage, unable to make out the audience because of the bright lights in my eyes. I gave the half-hearted wave of a trespasser and squirmed for a few minutes. He pulled away slowly and I was so concerned that I fell into a deep sleep within two and one-half minutes.

LESSON: Be careful, not all birds fly.

Day 49

A Hard Rain
[October 30]

I endured a rainy, blustery night, verifying the seventeen holes I have in my light tarp. With the high number of trucks I saw last night, I wasn't looking forward to pedaling on the shoulderless Highway 96 in the rain, but as I began my rainy morning ride, a two-foot shoulder developed.

The first couple of trucks that passed provided a refreshing wakeup call as their air surge lifted my raincoat and fleece and sprayed me with cool rainwater. Riding in the rain was a stark contrast to my other forty-eight days of sunshine, and it was actually quite peaceful. In the rain you don't look around as much at

MISSOURI

Springfield

Carthage
Nixa
Republic
Ava
Mark Twain Nat'l Forest

Mark Twain Nat'l Forest

Eleven Point River

Mark Twain Nat'l Forest
W. Plains
Alton
Doniphan

Kennett
Gobler

Mississippi River

ILLINOIS

KENTUCKY

TENNESSEE

KANSAS

ARKANSAS

Still pedaling hard, moving through the oak-covered hills of the Ozarks.

the scenery, and you get lost in your own little world of thoughts.

Fifteen miles down the road I came to a cozy gas station/restaurant. As I dug in my handlebar bag for my wallet and began to shake off the rain, a jolly old man ran out to me from his booth and jokingly asked, "How did you enjoy your little sleep last night?"

I laughed and shook his hand realizing he was the mysterious man in the truck—the potential drive-by-shooting guy. I talked with him, his old cronies, and Linda, the shop owner, for an hour, promising to drop them a postcard at the trip's completion.

I continued south and east, amazed at how quickly the prairie lands of Kansas were transformed into the oak-covered foothills of the Ozark Mountains. At a stop in the little town of Republic, I met two crazy young bucks named Jim and Jake who were just out of high school. Though they were mechanics by trade, the focus of their life seemed to be drinking beer and chasing women.

As the rain alternated between dribbles and buckets, the scenery became more and more beautiful. I appeared to have traded the flat terrain and high winds of Kansas for the rolling hills, mountains, and calmer breezes of Missouri. I passed beautiful reddish brown oaks and graceful, muscular horses.

A bizarre incident occurred as I headed east on Highway 14. I stopped for a break on the country road and noticed a lady and her daughter looking out of their window at me. I thought I would be soon answering the same questions I have for the last forty-eight days, but as they rushed out of their house, they stopped thirty feet from me.

The young girl cautiously touched a yellow Lab that appeared to be sleeping in the grass. The girl screamed and the mother covered her face with a towel and began wailing. They both slowly backpedaled from the lifeless dog toward the house, and as they did, a heavy rain began to fall. I watched in a daze as the huge raindrops fell on the dead dog. I stared blankly with a mouthful of unchewed granola bar, listening to the rain beat against my baseball cap. Too sad.

On a much more uplifting note, I was lucky enough to connect with my Aunt Miriam and Uncle Walt just before they departed for a trip to Michigan. They drove thirty miles north from Branson and intersected my route at the highway exit town of Nixa.

I had pedaled hard for the last five hours, battling the numerous hills, in order to meet them at our agreed upon time. It was strange to see familiar faces after spending so much time in my rainy little dream world. It was great to stop pedaling, to remove my soggy, moldy eight-day-old socks and throw on my sandals, to put on a dry fleece and shorts, and to talk four hours with two cool people I actually knew and grew up with.

LESSON: This morning, like every morning, I scrolled through my bike computer to glance at yesterday's total mileage and average speed. I rode 101 hard-earned miles yesterday. But with the press of one button, I reluctantly make that total disappear as I reset the instrument for the present day. Yesterday's mileage total does not help me climb hills today, does not help me ride nine hours in rain, does not force me to keep pedaling when I become fatigued, and does not contribute to today's mileage. Each day is a proving ground.

Day 50

Talking to Myself
[October 31]

It was very much a blue-collar day. The American flag in Nixa was flapping in the wind, which, of course, was blowing from my direction of travel—east.

I battled the headwind and Ozark Mountains for the entire day, picking a rural route in which I never saw a town or village. I was amazed at the number of small churches scattered throughout the hills, many of them clustered in areas with seemingly no population to support them.

The scenery rolled on and on, grassy pastures set against reddish brown oak forests. It seemed each individual oak tree sported a slightly different hue, ranging from red to dark brown, giving the hillsides a textured, patchwork look.

The Ozark hills were better suited to me physically. I am more of a sprinter than an endurance guy, so I was able to motor up the short steep hills quite quickly. By the time I was ready for an oxygen mask and a cold beer, the hill would be over and I was enjoying a beautiful autumn descent. The only problem was that there were 45,000 of these hills on my route

The Ozarks are this country's oldest mountains.

across Missouri!

Isolated rides like today—in which I had virtually no human contact—are a blessing. Rarely in our fast-paced days do we ever budget an hour or two to just think. One of the primary concepts I've learned on this trip deals with self-talk.

We all speak to ourselves at a rate of hundreds of words per minute, most of it a long, intermingled, in-terrelated, undisciplined string of garbage. If a truck passed extremely close to me, especially on a wide-open stretch with no traffic, I would find myself crafting an ugly, pissed-off, cursing speech in my mind that would have been satisfying to deliver to the driver.

As this trip, composed of several weeks of eight-hour solo rides and filled with more self-talk than most busy Americans experience in five years, has pro-gressed, I've developed a finer screen for weeding out silly, negative, debilitating self-talk.

I know that approximately one out of every one hundred and fifty drivers is either clueless or a wiener, so when one of those yahoos crosses my path, I accept him as just a minor portion of the population. I refuse to let him negatively control my mood for more than thirty seconds. For every one of this type, there are 149 other solid, courteous drivers that give waves, thumbs up, and supportive honks.

I've come to a greater awareness of self-talk and how directly it affects my moods. It's no wonder people constantly have their TVs and radios turned on, at-tempting to drown out and override words, thoughts, and scenarios from their worst enemy—themselves.

I spent a restful night in a thick forest of oaks, well tapped out from the wind and hills. The moisture was thick in the air, so I thankfully set up the light tarp over my head between two oaks. The rain and wind blasted me at three o'clock the next morning.

LESSON: Be aware of self-talk and discipline its flow.

Good Energy

[November 1]

The rain stopped just as I awoke at dawn. I packed away my moist gear and headed out.

Within a couple of miles I crossed Bryant Creek and enjoyed the view of its clear waters. It's wonderful to have crossed so many beautiful rivers on this trip, to enjoy all the diversity in their water volume, clarity, surrounding plant life, and unique smells. But it is also interesting to witness how they are so similar—each with its repeated cycle of riffle, run, and pool—and to guess the prime holding areas for trout.

I've been fortunate to have fly fished on many incredible stretches of rivers and to have experienced many wonderful times with friends. Rivers are so deeply ingrained in my being that my ashes will someday be dispersed in the lakes and streams that have stirred my soul over the years—the Buller in New Zealand, a highland lake in Tasmania, the Speil River in Alaska, several streams in northern Michigan, the Arkansas in Colorado, and the clear waters off a key in Belize.

I continued east, working my way into the colorful oaks of the Mark Twain National Forest. By 10 A.M. the calm, overcast day turned a bit blustery, with a steady crosswind from the south that made the cycling a bit more difficult. At a remote crossroads I found a small, old general store and inhaled a couple of cans of ravioli and crushed pineapple.

As I ate, I experienced a sensation similar to a Bigfoot sighting. An old man with no socks, shoes, or shirt—and sporting old jeans and a wild foot-long white beard—jogged out of the forest on a small two-track to a rusty mailbox across the road from me. As

The Mark Twain National Forest in southern Missouri encompasses nearly 1.5 million acres, including 63,000 acres of federally designated wilderness.

ride

he grabbed his mail, I gave him a quick wave. He nodded and quickly retreated back into the thick woods.

I finally reached some relatively flat terrain as I approached West Plains, but my southern heading placed me right into the teeth of the wind. I was a little frustrated with my progress in the hills and wind, so I continued pedaling into the dark, making some solid time as I reached Alton.

A lunch break in the Mark Twain National Forest of the Ozark Mountains.

Working as hard as I could over the last three hours had me sweaty and smelling like a caribou. At a local store, a pickup pulled next to me and I began speaking with a friendly guy named Ted. He checked me out as our conversation progressed from generalities to route advice and funny stories. Finally he invited me to stay the night with his family.

Within thirty minutes I went from having a distinct body odor, wet gear, stinky clothes, no company, and a savage thirst to a warm shower, dried tarp and sleeping bag, clothes in the washing machine, and a pleasant conversation over cold Budweisers with Ted, his wonderful wife, Carla, and spunky five-year-old Ana.

Ted was a true cowboy who worked on many of the cattle feedlots I had passed in Kansas. He and his family lived in a cozy house only a few blocks from the country home in which he grew up, surrounded by the Ozarks.

Ana and I engaged in a few fencing duels with her inflatable swords and throughout our conversation she gave us a fashion show of her Halloween costume and other play clothes. As I slumbered that night on their couch, I listened to the rain fall and wind blow. I felt pretty lucky.

During our conversation that night, I thanked Ted again for taking me into his home and explained how kind strangers had been to me compared to the treatment received by the down-and-out cyclist I had met a few days before. Ted said, "Nah, it's just about the energy people give off."

LESSON: Our individual energy fields vary as a function of our backgrounds, moods, and the lessons we've learned. As we cross paths with others, our fields either attract these people into our lives or repel them.

Day 52

Ropin' and Castin'
[November 2]

Ana helped me shave in the morning, and then we all enjoyed some great breakfast burritos prepared by Carla.

Last evening Ted had shown me his collection of guns, as well as an old bamboo fly rod his grandfather had left him. Over breakfast, we planned to exchange a bit of knowledge before I left. Instead of a briefcase filled with paperwork, Ted had a fancy case hanging next to his front door that contained his lasso, his essential business tool.

We headed outside, and before too long he had me whipping that thing around and roping a bucket we had placed twenty-five feet away. I reciprocated by rigging up his grandpa's old fly rod and sharing my hard-earned secrets. Ted was an expert with the bullwhip and he was quickly able to transfer some of those skills to throwing tight loops with the fly rod. He learned more quickly than did anyone I've ever met. Ted shared with me his plan to start an outfitting company where he would take clients horseback riding through the beautiful Ozark Mountains. I suggested he combine that with a little fly fishing on some of the local steams. I think we'll be seeing each other again before too long and sincerely hope I'll be one of his first customers.

Roping lessons from a pro.

I headed east with a slight tailwind and re-entered the Mark Twain National Forest. After thirteen miles of riding, I arrived at the wide, clear Eleven Point River, and as I walked along its banks, I wished I had my kayak with me. I continued riding over some of the same hilly terrain, stopping for lunch at the top of a small switchback from which there was a sweet panoramic view of the Ozarks. I watched a hawk grow smaller and smaller as he rode the convection currents.

My perfect day took a turn for the worse as a slow rain began to develop and a couple of thorns punctured my rear tire. My rear brakes were also out of adjustment, so I cut my ride short in Doniphan and performed a maintenance program on my bike in the expansive yard of a large church.

LESSON: Learning new skills from quality people allows you to take a piece of them with you forever.

The Stories of Old Men
[November 3]

I got a late start pedaling this morning, waiting until daylight to finish working on my bike. As I reached eastern Missouri near Poplar Bluff, the land predictably got flatter, but the southern wind became stronger and stronger in my face. I would rather have still been tangling with the mountains.

I had some wonderful conversations with friendly Missourians, the most memorable being with a retired rancher named Orville from the town of Harviell. At a small restaurant, I had asked a table of old dudes for some directional advice and immediately sensed how well respected this guy was by his buddies. He told me of wonderful trips he had taken out West, his favorite spot, like mine, being near Canon City, Colorado.

Near dusk I stopped for dinner at a small, dingy restaurant in Campbell. I was the only customer, but I talked awhile with two rough-looking waitresses, learning what the locals do for excitement and obtaining some key route advice. The blonde waitress said that I could ride in the dark on Highways 53 and 25 because they had shoulders, and she added that I could cross the Mississippi River on smaller Route 104 rather than on monster Highway 155.

She was from the tiny town of Gobler, directly on the route I was traveling, and she seemed pretty street smart. I left the character-filled plywood interior and began some relaxing night riding. Ten miles later on Highway 25 the road's shoulder disappeared, and after a cattle truck rattled me, I snuck into some deep grass between two cotton fields for the evening. I spent a relaxing night in the soft grass, spotting eight shooting stars and hoping the Gobler lady just forgot about this one small shoulderless stretch of road.

LESSON: Listen to the cool stories of old men.

Day 54

The Evil Troll from Gobler

[November 4]

Rough day today. I awoke to find that three big goat's head thorns had lodged in my rear tire and flattened it overnight. I was to meet Julia tomorrow for a weekend in Nashville, and she was bringing spare tubes and a heavy-duty touring tire for me.

At the moment, I was sporting a sissy sporting tire on my rear rim and it appeared to be paper-thin and have some type of thorn-attracting properties. My rear tube already boasted five patches. It would now have eight. I only had four patches left in my arsenal, but after this patch job I'd be dangerously down to just one.

I continued on Highway 25. There continued to be no shoulder on the road, and the truckers did not appreciate my route selection. I tested my own self-talk device, renaming my advice-giving waitress of last night the "Evil Troll from Gobler."

I arrived in the early morning in Kennett and enjoyed breakfast while sitting next to a nice old lady named Doris. We chatted and I learned of all her children and grandchildren. I headed out of Kennett, luckily finding a wide, black asphalt sidewalk that let me stay off the busy road.

The low sun cast long shadows on the dark-surfaced sidewalk, and traveling at 18 mph my front rim found an invisible curb. I catapulted over my handlebars eight feet onto the asphalt, cringing at the thought of what my front rim looked like. I assessed the damage to my rim, handlebars, handlebar bag, and pride. The rim had a nice kink but could be ridden on. I quickly straightened my handlebars, used cord to reattach my bag, widened my brakes to accommodate the new crinkle in my rim, and was on my way within ten minutes.

I worked hard into the wind, heading south off Highway 155 to reach my off-the-beaten-path bridge across the Mississippi River. Last night's waitress was now officially the "Evil Troll from Gobler" when I found the small bridge to be an abandoned ferry crossing. I thought of nothing but how this was a lesson in self-responsibility as I pedaled back north to the Highway 155 crossing and calculated that my mistake cost me twenty-five miles. I sure was glad I gave her a five-dollar tip on a four-dollar meal.

I finally reached the massive iron bridge that spanned the mighty Mississippi and led to Tennessee. I stopped at its highest point and marveled at the huge river. As I began pedaling to the other side, I felt the familiar hard thumps of another flat rear tire.

I walked my bike a half mile off the bridge and down a grassy hill off the busy highway. The puncture was a pressure flat characterized by a snake-bite-type double hole and would be difficult to patch with my single remaining patch. Joe Montana and Dwight Clark once completed a miracle reception for a touchdown in the NFL playoffs that was known as "The Catch." As I rode for another ten miles I thought I would forever remember this repair job as "The Patch," but the thought deflated just as my rear tire did and

The Mississippi River (Algonquian for "big water") is the largest river in North America, flowing 2,340 miles from Lake Itasca, Minnesota, to the Gulf of Mexico. From Cairo to New Orleans the river is generally 3,000 to 5,000 feet wide and 9 to 12 feet deep in the navigation channel.

the sun began to set. I was now ten miles from Dyersburg, Tennessee, with darkness approaching and no patches left.

Two small economy cars passed me, but in the distance I spotted a small pickup. I made eye contact with the driver, gave him the thumb, and he stopped. Luckily, I had a ride within thirty seconds of being off my bike. The man ended up being a die-hard Green Bay Packer fan and ex-cyclist. He had attempted to ride from Tennessee to Colorado ten years ago, but stopped after 300 miles because "it became too much work." I was supposed to pick Julia up at the airport tomorrow at 8 A.M., so he dropped me off at a rental car agency fifteen minutes before they closed.

I stuffed my bike into the trunk of the small compact car, drove to a restaurant, and wrote in my journal for five hours. I periodically talked with a dreamy, idealistic high-school girl as she cleared tables and mopped floors. I started my drive toward Nashville at 10:30 P.M., finally stopping at 1 A.M. on a backroad near a quarry pit where I curled up in my small car.

LESSON: Where you are in life and the people who surround you are a direct result of you and your actions. When life gets shitty, don't look for scapegoats, look in the mirror.

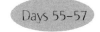

Days 55–57

Going Country

[November 5–7]

I somehow woke up to my wristwatch alarm clock at 6 A.M. and finished my drive to Nashville.

I don't have a strong affinity for cities, but Julia
and I had a great weekend. We started by taking a
horseback ride in the beautiful hills to the north of the
city. It was a colorful fall day, and it was relaxing for
just the two of us to ride without a guide and a string
of other horses.

As we finished our ride, the ranch hand and a
couple of his buddies were practicing rope tricks with
their lassos. We watched until we discovered that I had
locked the keys in the car. Fortunately my bike was
bungied in the open trunk and I was able to manhandle
a latch on the back seat and slither through to open
the doors.

Julia found a fine little restaurant that was re-
nowned for featuring upstart musicians and
songwriters. It was a cozy, intimate evening; our three-
foot-wide table was about three feet from five musicians playing acoustic guitars in a circle. They would
take turns, each playing and singing a song he had
written. It was easy to get lost in their songs as they
played their hearts out.

Several times I was in another world listening to
the lyrics as a performer sang his guts out and I'd turn
to Julia and see tears welling up in her eyes. We left

the Bluebird Café and strolled in the warm air to a bookstore where we found another collection of artists performing and hoping to hit the big time.

About the time you'd begin feeling a bit sorry for these performers singing their hearts out in obscurity, someone would let you know that that Ricky Skaggs or some other star had recorded the song you just heard. So even if we didn't recognize their names, their songwriting was touching thousands of people.

On Saturday we indulged in a few college football games on TV and then spent the evening at the Grand Ole Opry. The place oozed with tradition and we enjoyed the mix of current country phenoms intermingled with old-timers in their tacky sequin-studded outfits. My favorite moment was when Little Jimmy Dickens, an old dude who stood four-foot-something, came out with a flashy costume and a guitar that covered half his body. He quickly got the place fired up. All the performers seemed so happy to be performing there.

On our final day in the area we headed south to Murfreesboro and visited the Stones River National Battlefield and Cemetery, site of a brutal three-day Civil War battle. You get a hollow feeling in your gut when you learn of the strategies of the commanders, the tales of the participants, the piles of amputated arms and legs in the aftermath, how both sides suffered through freezing nights without fires so they wouldn't give away their positions, and the tally of 23,000 dead.

Although this day it was sunny and seventy degrees, you could imagine what it felt like for the young men on the cold December night before the battle, hearing the other side's band playing and knowing a bloody day was to follow.

The Battle of Stones River, fought between December 31, 1862 and January 2, 1863, came to an indecisive end, but on January 3 the Confederate forces withdrew and the Union army occupied Murfreesboro on January 5.

LESSON: Americans today are blessed with the gifts of freedom our forefathers often paid for in the form of mangled bodies and blood.

Still, when you look out over a battlefield cemetery and visualize the death and destruction that took place, you wonder how two sides can be so divided that they would allow the grotesque process of war to be a method of resolving the difference.

Day 58

On the Road Again

[November 8]

I woke a little kinked up after having bedded down in the "Chevy Cavalier Hotel." Last night I had driven the rental car until one in the morning. I parked in an abandoned parking lot next to a cotton field and went to sleep. Pieces of cotton had accumulated in scattered piles around the parking lot, and in the early morning's light they looked way too much like snow.

I headed back toward the Missouri border where a few days ago the flat bike tire had forced me to hitchhike. I found the exact mile marker, walked my bike into the woods, and locked it up. Being the freak I am, I had to start biking from the exact spot where I had stopped to ensure I bike every friggin' inch of this route.

An old classic named Ted drove me back to my bike in the rental car company's courtesy shuttle and told me old Civil War tales along the way—brothers fighting brothers, gunfire in peach orchards so thick that it appeared to be snowing from the falling blossoms. He even headed into the woods with me to verify that my bike was in solid working order before he left me in the middle of nowhere.

Before he left, he shook my hand and looked me deep in the eye and said, "I ain't worried about you. Remember to watch the other guy."

Handling all the logistical stuff took forever, and I didn't begin riding until four in the afternoon. I followed the advice Ted had given me and traveled the backroads south of Dyersburg. I had a few options to head across Tennessee, so at a gas station I asked the input of a few different truckers.

My chance to cover a few more miles before dark ended when I met a young trucker named John who had an endless supply of hilarious stories. He made it his mission to enlighten me with the ways of the trucker, telling tales, showing me around his huge rig, and explaining maximum loads, weigh stations, and the use of multiple log books to fool officials.

A couple of good ol' boys from Mississippi, who had bagged a monstrous eleven-point buck on their recent hunting trip, joined us. The huge buck was like a good-ol'-boy magnet, transforming the parking lot into a party. I finally snuck out and pedaled an hour in the dark on Highway 12's wide shoulder. I salvaged twenty-eight miles for the day before I found an abandoned farmhouse on a dirt road and threw my sleeping bag down in the overgrown lawn.

LESSON: Remember to watch the other guy.

Mind Games

[November 9]

Began the day with unbelievably ideal riding conditions—flat ground and no wind. I cruised a quick
thirty-five miles into Jackson, Tennessee, and as I
headed toward a grocery store, I struck up a conversation with a man and we ended up shopping through
the aisles together. His name was Ernest and my bike
brought back wonderful memories for him of his time
cycling in Europe with his five best buddies. He was
stationed with the Army in Germany but stayed for
an extra two years to goof off. They had a great time.

As he said, "Back then I had my 'fro grown long
and proud, and those German girls thought I was
Michael Jackson. Of course I never told them no
different."

On my way to Savannah, Tennessee, I branched
off to Routes 199 and 224 and enjoyed the peaceful,
rolling, oak-covered farmland. The hundred-foot hills
occurred so frequently they were almost unnoticeable.

I spent a couple of hours pedaling in a daze, hyp-
notized by the old, weathered barns, green pastures,
and distant hills. As the sun dipped low in the sky, I
crossed a big iron bridge over the Tennessee River and
entered the old, majestic southern town of Savannah.
I interrupted my fast-paced pedaling to ease slowly
through town, enjoying the old historic courthouse. I
then cranked it hard to finish off my 100-miler before
the sun set.

I love the end of each day; the competitive juices
always begin to flow when I realize the setting sun and
hilly terrain are battling against me to take away my
100-mile day. My goal is always to hit 80 miles and
then begin the 10-mile countdown until I reach 90.

At 90 I try to sprint the last 10 miles knowing that I have the competition reeling against the ropes.

LESSON: Mentally condition yourself to finish your competition off when you have him faltering, whether the competition is a goal, a project, an opposing team, or your own mental block. As McDonald's Ray Kroc said, "When you see your competition is drowning, ram a live hose down his throat."

Day 60

Death of a River
[November 10]

I shared a barnyard last night with a feisty quarter horse. I slept behind an old green barn that was adjacent to a ten-acre fenced field. The horse had the large field with tons of fresh, juicy grass to tromp through, but he decided to spend the entire night within ten feet of me. Like an alarm clock, each hour he blasted a loud, deep, throaty croak that sounded more like a hog than a horse.

Each day in Tennessee has been exactly the same — the temperature soars to seventy-five degrees, the skies are cloudless, and the air humid and thick. During the evenings the air cools and a thick dew covers all my gear. Getting up each morning is like waking to a light rain shower.

I pedaled ten miles over misty hills until I arrived at the village of Olivehill and stopped at an old general store with "H.O. Smith & Sons" above the door.

The H.O. Smith &
Sons family store
in Olivehill,
Tennessee.

Walking through the door I stepped back in time. Two old men were lazily kicked back in old chairs in front 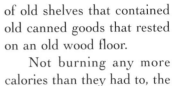 of old shelves that contained old canned goods that rested on an old wood floor.

Not burning any more calories than they had to, the boys slowly, courteously nodded at me as I entered. I grabbed a few items off the shelves and then broke the ice, starting a conversation with the more energetic of the two. Forty minutes later I had made two new buddies and completely destroyed my early morning start.

By the time I got my butt off one of those old chairs, I had learned that these gentlemen were the "sons" in H. O. Smith & Sons, that the family business started in 1920, and that one had been a food inspector in Oregon and Idaho for twenty years. The boys came back to take care of their parents, and the hardest thing they ever did was sell off the family 400-acre farm because they could no longer profitably run it.

But we spent most of the time talking about fishing, and I loved to hear their boyhood tales of catching tons of smallmouth bass and catfish in nearby Indian Creek. I then felt my guts get ripped out as they described how loggers over the last fifty years had clear-cut the surrounding hills. The logging had allowed tons of soil to run into the creek, covering spawning areas and destroying the five species of fish that used to flourish in their favorite stream.

They don't waste their time fishing Indian Creek anymore, but instead travel to a reservoir formed by the damming of the Tennessee River. I wanted to puke. They described to me their favorite childhood fishing hole beneath the "old arch bridge," which was now

ride

filled with sand, and urged me to check it out as I headed east. A mile and a half later, I had a hollow feeling as I snapped a shot of the old bridge, and beneath it, the shallow, lame bend in the river that was once a deep, cold pool, and a magical place for two young boys.

I hauled up a 600-foot climb as I approached Waynesboro and was reminded what it's like to have burning quads again. I crossed the Green River, pausing as always, giving homage to the river gods.

I arrived in Lawrenceburg, weaseled my way through the traffic on the nonexistent shoulder, and coasted into a gas station. A passing car noticed me, quickly turned around, and pulled up next to me. I had a lengthy conversation with this local businessman and fellow cyclist, fully realizing my 100-mile day was setting with the sun.

The shorter autumn days were beginning to put a kink in my social life. I pedaled like a madman around Pulaski, utilizing the spacious and monstrous bypass that edged far beyond the small city. They must have some aggressive growth plans for the town in the next decade, or perhaps I missed something.

Construction west of Fayetteville was congesting traffic and the shadows were growing larger. I snuck around the barrels and had 15 miles of newly paved two-lane road to myself. I reached Fayetteville at dark with 101 miles registering on my bike.

I ate dinner at a homey ma-and-pa restaurant next to an extremely nice retired Air Force couple. When the man was a young buck, he planned on riding his unicycle from Louisiana to California, but he was overcome with common sense and the trip never materialized. Several years ago this couple found a young man with two mules sleeping in a field on their 100-acre farm. He was traveling to Ohio to attend a religious gathering, by mule, and was utilizing some of the same money-saving, soul-enriching lodging facilities that I was. They offered me a place to stay, but I had already scouted out a cozy cotton field just down a side road from the restaurant.

Lesson: Our country's natural resources are gifts that benefit us recreationally, emotionally, and spiritually. We can't afford to enjoy these gifts without regard for their health. We slowly damage our souls each time we canoe, kayak, raft, or fish a river, take note of the damage man is inflicting, and still decide to do nothing.

Day 61

Last Climb

[November 11]

Emerged from my cozy cubbyhole—nestled between two fallen trees in the middle of a cotton field—surrounded by a light, mystical mist. I pedaled today at a calmer, more relaxed pace, enjoying the small clear creeks I crossed and the rust- and red-tinged oak forests.

Today I was indulging in my fifty-eighth day of sunshine on this now sixty-one-day-old trip. Just outside of Fayetteville, I spotted a cool old barn filled with racks of drying tobacco.

At midday I climbed probably my last real hill of the trip—2,000-foot Mount Sewanee. As I began the climb, I couldn't help reflecting on the 50,000 or so feet I've climbed on this trip. Each mountain and hill seemed to enrich the soul a bit. Each one humbled me, caused my legs to burn, and tempted me to quit. Yet

Mount Sewanee lies in the southern portion of the Cumberland Plateau. The plateau has extensive forests and is impassable in many parts because of the rugged terrain.

each also provided me with a moment at the summit in which I felt like God was unveiling his expansive masterpiece. I never took myself too seriously when I finally reached the top, even if I was able to hammer the climb. I remembered reading that climbing a mountain is not just the result of our own doing. For each step we take pushing down, the mountain is also there pushing up.

I scooted 1,100 feet up the switchbacks in roughly thirty-five minutes, supported by toots from trucks along the climb. I was beginning to develop a greater fondness of truckers. A small number of the stubborn ones take a sick pleasure in passing dangerously close, even when there is no traffic in the oncoming lane. A small number of the ornery ones enjoy stomping on their accelerator just as they reach me so that their diesel engines belch a deep, loud moan—jarring me out of my peaceful thoughts and making my heart skip a beat.

But truckers are also the only ones on the road who can relate to this type of experience. Only they understand the long hours on the road, the energy expended on a long uphill climb, the sometimes subtle and sometimes dramatic terrain changes as you move from state to state, the sameness and nasty food of convenience stores, the keen awareness of the day's weather and how it affects your day, the massive open spaces of this country, and the flow of your mind as you spend hours and hours speaking to no one but yourself.

Just as the climb began to get difficult, it was over. At the top, I cruised around the shops of the small village of Sewanee and briefly explored the campus of the University of the South. The beautiful old stone church and the small, low-key organic fruit shop gave the tiny town a homey, comfortable feel. Along my route today I asked approximately twelve people about a twenty-five mile section of Route 156 that I planned on taking south out of Sewanee, rather than being forced onto larger state routes as I headed toward Chattanooga. Not one person had even heard of the road or knew of its existence. I decided that could be a good sign or bad one. It ended up being a great sign, as I enjoyed an empty road that carved through oak forests across roller-coaster-like terrain.

Eight miles into Route 156 my scenic solitude was broken by a passing bicyclist. As a man in an old, classic road bike passed I jokingly commented that he hurt my feelings and made me feel inadequate by passing my bloated bicycle and me at such a high speed. He laughed and we rode the next five miles together. He was entirely too easy to talk with and we had much in common. His name was Ken and he was the head football coach at the small college in Sewanee. It was one of those nongrowth conversations, since we held many of the same views on topics like the balance between college athletics and academics, work ethic in today's students, and goal setting. As he did a quick U-turn to head back for practice, I laughed at myself for mistakenly concluding what an incredibly refined, insightful, and sharp guy Ken was—when actually the correct judgment should have been that we held the same opinion on a wide range of topics.

As I headed south on 156 my views turned ugly several times as I reached portions of the thick oak forest that were owned by a local hunting club and completely clear-cut. As I neared South Pittsburg, I screamed down one of the steepest and most serpentine sections of the trip, losing virtually all of the elevation I gained at Mount Sewanee in a wacky, tight-turning two miles. The Ozark, Cumberland, and Appalachian mountains of Missouri and Tennessee did not come close to the high peaks and 3,500-foot climbs of Idaho and Colorado, but the grades in which they rose were comparable. And the positives of having shorter climbs, less severe temperatures at the lower elevations and latitudes, and no snow made them a great time.

LESSON: After having a conversation with someone who shares many of your beliefs and values, it is very difficult to not say to yourself, "That dude is one of the most highly intelligent people I have ever met."

Day 62

Restless Souls
[November 12]

I spent the morning tooling around the outskirts of Chattanooga. As I came upon a fireworks outlet on Highway 24 featuring the largest, gaudiest, brightest, electricity-sucking neon sign I have ever seen, I remembered why I preferred the scenery and peacefulness of my rural routes.

At 10:30 A.M. I pulled into a Big Boy Restaurant to belly up to their all-you-can-eat breakfast buffet. My nine trips to the buffet and hour-and-a-half stay guaranteed the franchise a loss on my visit.

I continued on my way, crossing the Tennessee River, humming some related country tune by Alabama, and thinking how close I was to Georgia, my final state. I rode along the southern shore of Nickajack Lake—a dam-created bulge in the Tennessee River. In the bright sun I managed to spot two or three bass hanging motionless along the rocky, oak-lined shoreline in six feet of water, though I now scouted much less intently than I did when I was sporting my fly rod in order not to torture myself.

The experience of spotting beautiful fish in lakes and rivers on this trip, watching them rise for a bug or swerve for a nymph — without my fly rod — gave me brutal flashbacks of my post-college years of playing flag football. After being fortunate enough to play strong safety in college and being allowed to regularly tee off on slippery wide receivers, pulling the flag after an opponent made a catch in flag football was unsatisfying. Colorful rainbow trout rising during a caddis hatch needed a well-presented barbless artificial firmly planted in their jaw just as cocky wide receivers lurching for an errant pass needed a well-placed hit somewhere between their helmet and shoulder pads.

I took one of my patented cold-ravioli-in-a-can breaks at the side of a small two-lane road that ran parallel to monstrous Interstate 24. As I opened my can, a burly, bearded man in a red Jeep gave me a long ten-second stare as he slowly turned down a two-track that wound into the woods. Minutes later I heard a loud blast as he emptied his muzzleloader in the oak-covered hills. When I began my second gourmet entrée of Beefaroni, the red Jeep returned, I gave him a wave, and he pulled up to check out my story.

I must have the look of a person who's either an alcoholic or perpetually thirsty because after a few minutes of lively conversation, this stranger, like several before him, offered me a cold beer out of his cooler. Sam told me how all his relatives since his great-great-grandfather have been buried in the Raccoon Mountains that surrounded us, indicated on my map the various movements of the Rebels and Yankees during the Battle of Chattanooga, and discussed his views on the health of the Tennessee River. I was fortunate to have crossed paths with another classic.

As I continued through Chattanooga, I went against Sam's advice and took a route with no shoulder that hugged a rocky cliff face. Most locals wouldn't consider riding a bike more than five miles and often underestimate which roads are at least halfway safe on a bicycle — so this was not the first piece of advice I had blown off. Bad move. The road was a bit more

One of the better tailwater trout streams in Tennessee is the Hiwassee River, about an hour north of Chattanooga. Recent stream management improvements are likely to make this state Scenic River even better.

hairy than I anticipated. At one point, a gust of wind removed my beat-up baseball cap and left it lying behind me in the middle of the lane—on a tight bend. Being a sentimental fool and hopelessly attached to the gear that had gotten me this far, I did a quick retreat into the blind corner to retrieve it. Fortunately, I scooped it up and moved back safely to the right side of the road just as a station wagon whizzed by at 60 mph. Moments of divine intervention like that along the road led me to believe I was on a mission from God to finish this thing off in one piece.

I hauled up a couple of steep hills to finish my short ride and headed to the historic Chickamauga and Chattanooga National Military Park. I stopped by the fancy visitor center, pushed the button for the automatic door, and then discovered that the place was closed for the day. As the sun went down, I scouted among the beautiful forests and fields for a place to sleep for the night. I then returned to the visitor center to place a phone call and found a couple of police officers and park rangers scurrying around with flashlights. As I chatted on the phone they looked suspiciously at the vagabond bike guy; I was too dense to realize that earlier I had set off their alarm system when I hit the automatic door button.

As I laid out my tarp and sleeping bag for the night, I heard strange noises in the nearby woods. I picked up the rhythmic pattern of four people shoveling sand—though I had just moments earlier traveled through the exact location and knew no one was out there. Thirty-four thousand men gave their lives on the battlefield where I slept—in a war in which many of them were not comfortable conceptually. As I drifted to sleep, my mind wandered—wondering if troubled souls still lingered in these woods and fields, digging entrenchments, digging graves.

LESSON: Listen to the advice of crusty old locals.

More Killing Fields

[November 13]

Greeted the day to the sight of an old lady power-walking through the wooded trails where I slept. She enthusiastically wished me a good morning as I wiped the sleep drool off my chin. The battlefield was a strange place—unbelievably beautiful green fields, thick forests, rolling hills—but unfortunately the site of the slaughter of way too many lives.

I met a cool dude named Pat Riley from San Antonio who felt the same vibes from the eerie beauty of the well-preserved battlefield. We philosophized about the irrational, but never-ending, presence of war in this world as we checked out the line-up of cannons (killing machines) they had on display.

I spent hours riding through the different sections of the battlefield, learning of the little skirmishes and major brawls. During the battle, a miscommunication on the part of the Union's command left a gap in their lines. At the exact moment this hole developed, the Rebels coincidentally attacked that exact section of the line. It was the turning point of the entire battle—sometimes it's good to be lucky.

I positioned myself in the thick woods at the precise section where the grossly outnumbered Union soldiers viewed an entire division of Confederates charging across a field directly at them. The field and woods

Monument to the courageous 2nd Minnesota Brigade.

TENNESSEE

Chattanooga

N. CAROLINA

Chickamauga and
Chattanooga
Military Park

Appalachian
Mountains

Blue Ridge
Mountains

Chattahoochee
Nat'l Forest

Pushing hard for
the Atlantic
Ocean.

Chattahoochee
Nat'l Forest

Winder

ALABAMA

Atlanta

Winder

S. CAROLINA

Savannah River

Macon

Sylvania

GEORGIA

Savannah

Tybee Island

are little changed from that day, and you could imagine what a ghastly feeling it was to see hundreds of howling enemy soldiers with shining bayonets sprinting towards you—knowing you didn't have a prayer.

I spent a lot of time at the top of Snodgrass Hill, a place where Union soldiers fell back after the Confederate breakthrough and bravely defended their position. Markers and monuments erected after the war by veterans of the battle were found all over the battlefield—but the most moving to me depicted the courageous efforts of the 2nd Minnesota Brigade.

Despite valorous efforts, there was nothing glamorous about this war. Terror-filled screams from ugly hand-to-hand combat, beautiful horses gasping as they lay mutilated on the battlefield, moans and cries from dying soldiers…those should be the sounds we associate with the Civil War—not some romantic version of "Dixie."

At midday I left Chickamauga, grateful I was able to gain a new perspective, thankful for the bravery of the fallen soldiers. In the small town of Chickamauga, I stopped at a grocery store to stock up and met an eccentric old man named Mike with a bright white, bushy beard. He was riding an old green Schwinn Varsity and saw me packing my panniers full of food. He looked at me as though he had a story to tell. And he did. He told me of his backbreaking construction work on the suspension bridge in Savannah, Georgia, of his myriad family problems, and of his belief in simplicity. Even when he was discussing hardships, he seemed to have a big picture of what it all meant.

I continued south and east, pedaling up a nice grade to a small mountain pass called Shipp's Gap—the sight of another Civil War skirmish. I finally called it a day, stopping at a wonderful rolling field near Snake Creek in the Chattahoochee National Forest. The grass was soft and a formation of geese flew overhead. Life was good. I watched as a subtle fog one foot off the ground slowly grew into a humongous, misty, twelve-foot wall of cloud—just as the sun began to set.

Union casualties at Chickamauga numbered 16,179 killed, wounded, and missing; Confederate casualties were some 18,000.

LESSON: Never confuse the selfless, heroic actions of soldiers in war with glamour. War sucks.

Dear Sweet Little Friends

[November 14]

I awoke in the same dense fog I'd gone to bed with last night. Though the sky above was flawless, I was unable to see more than ten feet in front of me. Since I couldn't safely ride until the thick stuff burned off, I kicked back in the dewy puddles of my tarp and began reading a novel called *Co. Aytch: A Confederate's Memoir of the Civil War* by Sam R. Watkins that I purchased at Chickamauga. I became lost in the words written by a young Confederate soldier detailing his four years of battle as a member of the First Tennessee Regiment.

The man wrote a real book—one describing the war through the eyes of a common foot soldier not from the perspective of some fancy decorated general who "fought" the war off the front line in a comfortable officer's tent. He told of frightened soldiers shooting their fingers off in battle in order to bow out of the fight, of men with their lower jaws shot off still attempting to speak, of injured friends dictating letters to their mothers moments before they died in battle.

The sun finally broke through the fog, allowing me to dry my wet gear and finally trudge through the field back to the rural road. I entered the small village of Villanow and checked out the old general store dating back to the mid-1800s. Everything I saw now—the old store, wooded hills, open fields, ragged, aged barns— I saw in the context of the Civil War. My mind wandered as I replayed the words of the young Rebel soldier.

My clean vegetarian diet of the past few years was now just a dim memory. I would now arrive at a grocery store and inhale three powdered jelly-filled donuts as soon as I entered the building, ram two chocolate éclairs down my throat as I walked the aisles, pound down a half-gallon of corn syrupy Sunny Delight imitation orange juice, and start into my eight-pack of double-chocolate Pop-Tarts before I reached the cash register. I would then pathetically look at the cashier, white powder caked in the corners of my mouth, avoiding direct eye contact, and like a penitent in a Catholic confessional, give her a laundry list of the items not in the cart that needed to be rung up. Early in the trip, I would then ashamedly walk to my bike, load the granola bars and Beefaroni into my panniers, and comment to myself what an undisciplined, unhealthy, pitiful, namby-pamby I was.

But now, being a road-tested chowhound, I realized the ugly empty calories were a necessity—just part of the fuel I threw in my overactive furnace. I balanced them with healthy, slow-burning fuel. Now I thoroughly enjoyed these unhealthy morsels and relished every moment—fully aware that this pedaling-induced, ultra-fast metabolism I had created would soon fade as I would be forced to seatbelt myself back in front of a computer and telephone.

I traveled down scenic Route 411 enjoying the calm country farms, oak-lined hills, and clear skies. I found the road shoulders in Georgia scattered with cotton from passing trailers—as well as scattered with a morgue scene of dead possums, raccoons, snakes, owls, squirrels, dogs, cats, and chickens.

Night came quickly on this fog-shortened day, and I was forced to stop near Funkhouser, Georgia. I slid into a small orchard of apple trees, laid out my tarp, and sensed the clear sky quickly sucking away the last of the day's warmth.

LESSON: This trip is entirely too short and I will greatly miss many of my newfound friends who I must unfortunately part with at trip's end. I will not be able to list all their names, but they know who there are and they know the magical, self-indulgent times we spent together. Farewell Little Debbie snack cakes, powdered raspberry-filled donuts, fudge brownies with nuts at the Casey's convenience store chains, Hostess apple, blueberry, and cherry pies, double-chocolate and frosted-raspberry Pop-Tarts, Kudos chocolate-covered granola bars, and the rest of your little naughty brothers and sisters on the junk food shelves.

Day 65

Frozen Balmex

[November 15]

Frigid nighttime temperatures and nippy morning rides have returned. In life, I've always tried to practice delayed gratification—working hard to accomplish crappy, boring, painful, or difficult tasks before indulging in more enjoyable ones. On this trip I didn't have the choice. The most unpleasant tasks of the day always came first thing in the morning—when I was forced to exit my sleeping bag cocoon and enter the brutality of the cold outer world.

These same ugly steps were performed each day with minor variations: I would sit upright, slide out of my sleeping bag, feel the twenty-eight-degree air spank me, throw on a fleece as quickly as possible, reach under the tarp for my frozen-solid biking shoes, stand up like a crickity old man, tend to nature's callings, grab the frozen tube of Balmex Diaper Rash Ointment, squirt a frozen line of the nasty stuff in my hand and apply it to every part of my anatomy that touched the bike seat, think to myself "this sucks," step into my constricting, nonventilated biking shorts (ending eight hours of free blood flow and comfort), pack up my gear with frozen fingers, and reset my bike computer. Good morning world, I'm ready to pedal.

At midmorning I came to the town of Canton—an almost ideal town with brick buildings and warm citizens. I needed to send a twenty-page fax so I began scouting for the right place to begin my groveling. I chose a refurbished old brick warehouse occupied by a number of law offices. I thought these people must have some soul or they wouldn't have bothered to restore the cool old structure. The receptionist was unbelievably nice, considering my unshaven state and the Balmex residue on my hand as I handed her my journal to fax. She refused to let me pay for the long document.

As I continued through town, a lack of directional signs forced me to ask directions—since mistakes on a bike are much more painful and time consuming than those in car. I spotted a lady on her knees, gardening in front of a beautiful home. Her back was toward me, so to warn of my approach, I coughed as I trudged across her front lawn. She didn't hear me. I was quite close as I said, "Excuse me, ma'am." Startled, she whipped around, staring directly at the bright orange-and-yellow sunshine socks Julia had given me during the trip. I could tell one of three thoughts were running through her mind: With socks like that (1) this guy is a fruit loop, (2) this intruder is a girly man and I know I can take him if he attacks, or (3) this guy is probably harmless and it appears from his clothing selection that he needs all the help and instruction I can give. Whatever her take on me, she was extremely cordial and provided me with great directions.

I was heading east, attempting to stay way north of the traffic nightmares of Atlanta. As I neared Cumming, Georgia, I crossed paths with two messy, paint-covered commercial painters. We seemed to be drawn together, perhaps because we were the only grungy looking characters in the convenience store full of well-dressed professionals. We laughed and exchanged stories for the duration of the painters' short lunch break.

As I pushed on, I found that the roads on my map that appeared to be cute and out of the way were actually the home to continuous new strip-mall development. I longed for the familiar, quiet, picturesque country roads that in the past weeks had allowed me to hum along peacefully and occasionally pull into a soulful mom-and-pop store. This stretch seemed only to affirm our country's urban sprawl problem and the "McDonaldization" of America. Monstrous semis and pickups pulling fancy bass boats were passing dangerously close to me on these shoulderless roads. As I crossed Lake Lanier, it was difficult to absorb the beauty of the water since I was more concerned about not becoming a hood ornament.

Hungry as usual, I pulled off to grub at a small store. I talked with a friendly man outside the store for a few minutes and as we walked in together he shared my story with the rest of the store—whether I wanted him to or not. The clerks were extremely nice, giving me a few articles of free food and listening to my stories. As I left, I met the owner of the store and we exchanged life philosophies for a half-hour or so. Her strong eye contact and the effortless flow of our conversation gave me the weird sensation that I already knew her.

I pedaled until dark, reaching the town of Winder. I guess I was becoming a bit wiser—even though I was at 82 miles for the day and within striking distance of

100, the prospect of cycling another hour and a half in the dark (with no bike lights) seemed less appealing than it did a month ago. Though I'd rather have been out in the country, I settled for sleeping behind a white church. I stretched out on the concrete steps in its back yard, ate a can of cold ravioli, listened to sirens blare past Main Street, and read some more of my Civil War book.

Lesson : Life is good when you can accomplish the nastiest task of the day first.

Day 66

The Sound of One Hand Clapping
[November 16]

Perhaps it is inevitable that when you take a trip like this with the goal, in part, of finding yourself, you end up losing yourself instead. We've all met people who seem pretty confident they know where they stand on most every issue placed in front of them, but I think that comes from a pretty shallow inspection of those issues. And shallow opinions are rampant in a society in which we scurry around like dogs trying to make ends meet—never budgeting enough time in our busy lives to truly examine life.

Riding for eleven hours a day provides that time, and then some. And most of the time I end up a little more clueless on issues than I was before I started— but at least I had time to examine my thoughts clearly.

The more you learn, the more you discover how little you know.

Today my mind wandered from stirring questions like, "Where does earwax come from?" to assorted thoughts about religion. I stopped midmorning to shed clothing from my frosty early morning start and I happened to be in front of a church. As I sat in the church's front yard, using the ditch near the road as a backrest, I munched granola bars and attempted to suck in the weak morning rays. After a few minutes, a friendly looking man driving a small Chevette passed by me as he headed into the church parking lot, checking out my overstuffed hog of a bike and giving me a bit of eye contact. I glanced over my shoulder, and seeing him begin the fifty-yard walk across the parking lot toward me, I popped up and met him halfway.

He was a jolly, robust fellow—looking a lot like Friar Tuck from Robin Hood or the monk in those old Xerox copier commercials. After exchanging niceties, I respectfully tried to unload on this unsuspecting clergyman the question that had been buzzing through my head this morning—and not the one about earwax.

I presented him this scenario: There is an old woman in an isolated African village who lives a wholesome, exemplary life. She doesn't curse or lie. She takes in orphans of the village and provides them with food and clothing. She also knows nothing of Christianity, but is aware of a Creator and a Higher Energy. There also exists a bitter cyclist, who has torn a bloody swath across the U.S. He has brutally clubbed forty women and children to death with his bike pump. During his arrest and trial, he shows no remorse and is quite comfortable with the despicable life he has led. Two days before he is to be executed, a pastor helps him to realize his wicked, contemptible ways and find the Lord.

I asked my attentive, but grimacing listener, "Is the kind old lady going to hell, while the nasty bike pump murderer goes to heaven"?

"Yes," he answered.

I continued riding on another near perfect day. I wandered off Highway 15 and found Elder's Bridge — a beautiful, restored covered bridge. The original hand-hewn supporting beams were monstrous, and it was fascinating seeing how the modern craftsman attempted to preserve the character of the structure during the renovation. I then passed what I believe is my favorite road name of the trip — Lickskillet Road — on my way to the Oconee National Forest.

When I reached the small town of White Plains, I entered a small store with a wonderful twenty-foot handcrafted countertop. As the store staff observed my obscene eating patterns, I inquired about a backroad I hoped to catch twenty miles south near Sparta. When the crew heard I was heading towards Sparta, they cringed as though I was pedaling into an unstable military zone. They walked me back to meet the mechanic who understood all the backroads in the area, and he gave me the official approval to proceed. But he warned, "don't dillydally, keep pedaling."

The gracious owner then gave me a business card with her home phone in case I ran into trouble. I've been into some ugly portions of cities before, often unintentionally, and as I rode off I jokingly wondered, "How dangerous can rural Georgia be?"

When I reached Sparta I was a bit bothered by their neighbors to the north. Sparta's citizens were entirely black…and entirely friendly. If one listed all the items — physically, mentally, emotionally, psycho-logically — that blacks and whites have in common, the scroll would be endless. The potential cultural and minor physical differences would produce a list that was perhaps one millionth as long. Why, then, do we seem to always stress the extremely short list and mini-mize the infinitely long one?

I finished my 100 miles in the small crossroads of Mitchell at dusk. I immediately spotted a quiet church with a large back yard that had nighttime accommo-dations written all over it. My food inventory was absolutely at zero so I headed to the only small shop in town and loaded up. As I heaped two cans of pineapple, two cans of corn, two cans of ravioli, and a jumbo can of Beefaroni onto the counter, the old man at the register commented, "You must be stocking up."

"Definitely not," I told him. "I can't fit all of this on my bike, but I think I can polish most of it off tonight."

He laughed and I spent the next forty-five minutes talking with this ex-trucker-turned-shop-owner and one of his buddies.

LESSON: Deep introspection designed to answer questions often just leads to more unanswered questions.

Day 67

EMOTIONAl GOO
[November 17]

Although I was now in the southernmost portion of my route, nighttime temperatures were still dipping into the midtwenties. As I readied my gear for the morning ride, I began became an emotional ball of sentimental goo. I had roughly 160 miles remaining to reach the Atlantic Ocean, so today would most likely be my final long ride.

As I performed each morning task my sappy mind wandered—"This is about the last time I'll fold my tarp," "This may be the last time I'll stuff my sleeping bag," "This is about the last time I'll reset my bike computer...blah, blah." Have mercy.

I hauled as fast as I could today, zipping through the towns of Edgeville, Grange, and Midville. It was a strange sensation witnessing the last of the hills of northern Georgia flattening—much as the Rockies did in eastern Colorado. But this time there would not be another range to conquer at the end of this stretch of flat land. At midday I crouched at a newspaper dispenser to read the front page as I usually did—too cheap to buy one, of course. Usually I just discovered the most recent naughty thing Bill Clinton had done—but today I learned of the Leonid meteor shower that was to occur tonight. I felt blessed that my final night under the stars would be a nature show.

I cycled like a madman today and probably did not replenish as many calories as I should have. By the time I reached Sylvania at dusk I was light-headed and could feel myself fading. Since I was in seventh grade I've stuck to a pretty disciplined diet, knowing that healthy food provided the best energy source for me and simply made me feel good. And even though I've indulged in some less than wholesome snacks on this trip, I had not managed to break down and consume any McDonald's hamburgers. This evening, in my heavily bonked condition, I realized it was my very last chance to cross the line into junk food heaven. In less than ten minutes, I swallowed four quarter-pounders with cheese almost without chewing—bringing back sensations I had not experienced for almost twenty years. I kicked myself as I pedaled away into the darkness, just as my gut told me it was still partially empty.

I finished up with a less than intelligent ride in the dark on Highway 21. I sprinted twenty miles until I came to a gas station in the village of Newington. I talked awhile with the owner, a relaxed sixty-year-old guy on a wooden stool. Three or four local boys then arrived and asked the man where he had been the last eight days. He sheepishly replied he had gotten married and the place erupted with handshakes, jokes, and general buffoonery. I enjoyed the merriment for a few minutes and then headed back into my own little world of peaceful darkness.

As I reached 100 miles, I headed two miles off the highway and found an ideal open field bordered by tall pine trees in which I could view most of the sky. Had I not read the article about the meteor shower, I would have been amazed at the twenty-five shooting stars that lit up the sky—instead I was slightly disappointed that sky was not ablaze with fireballs.

LESSON: During this ride I've been blessed to meet hundreds of wonderful people, most asking me the purpose of my journey. I would explain my love for fly fishing and kayaking, my emotional attachment to rivers, my realization of their economic importance to our economy in northwest Michigan, my desire for a challenge, and my connection with the quality and effective people at the Conservation Resource Alliance. I found, almost without exception, that their response was a function of geography. On the country roads within the states of Washington, Idaho, Utah, Colorado, and Kansas, the response would be a funky, Western "right on." As I traveled the rural routes of Missouri, Tennessee, and Georgia, their retort was a more bewildered "Oh, OK"—though behind their affirmation you could catch glimpses of their true thought process which varied from "Boy, if you want some exercise I've got a ditch that needs digging" to "Man, how about for your next ride you raise funds to put new siding on my double-wide trailer."

Land's End

[November 18]

My final day had arrived. My ass was happy, my heart was sad.

I rode in early morning temperatures of around twenty-seven degrees on empty Highway 21—stopping once to shed my cycling shoes and warm my stiff feet with my hands. The road was so barren that at 10:30 I was able perform a quick striptease on the shoulder—shedding tights in favor of shorts.

I had decided earlier in the trip that ideal riding conditions never existed—if I wasn't battling hills and mountains, there was always a headwind to contend with. But on my last day of pedaling, the perfect ride occurred—absolutely no wind and no elevation changes. These beatific conditions allowed me to cruise forty miles in just a couple of hours. I sailed along the wooded road, noticing the long Spanish moss that hung in large strands off thick tree branches. It was going to be strange to see the ocean again.

I entered the busy town of Garden City, just on the outskirts of Savannah—a fine test for my reflexes and city driving skills. Motorists were flying around with their heads cut off—zipping by within inches of my protruding panniers. It's always entertaining feeling the rushing air from a camper's large review mirror as it whizzes by your head at 60 mph. I could visualize the local newspaper headlines: "Cross-country Cyclist Lambasted by Pickup Truck Ten Miles from Final Destination."

A sidewalk finally developed and I eased my pace as I headed into Savannah. I granny geared along Bay Street, gazing at the monstrous cabled suspension bridge over the Savannah River and reconnecting in spirit with my old bearded buddy Mike from Chickamauga, who had his own blood and sweat invested in that structure.

I ceremoniously munched a Pop-Tart as I casually negotiated the cobblestone streets of the Historic District—checking out funky bars, classy restaurants, coffee shops, and the network of town squares that are a hallmark of Savannah. I made mental notes of places to investigate further with Julia and Amy Beyer, director of the Conservation Resource Alliance, when they arrived tomorrow for the weekend. But I cut the little tour short in order to finish business—I needed to dunk that front tire in the Atlantic Ocean.

I pedaled the final fifteen miles to Tybee Island and recalled just a few months ago scouring the map, looking for the farthest point east of Savannah to end my ride. I remembered attempting to picture in my mind what it would look like, envisioning the feelings I would have when I reached it. I crossed bridges over the Intracoastal Waterway and Turners Creek, smelling the salt air as I did in Washington State's Mukilteo State Park.

Heading onto the island, I crossed a long beautiful stretch of sea grass, wondering if this picturesque grassland prompted founders to call the nearby city Savannah. I crossed a final bridge—one that seemed to belong on a postcard—complete with colorful shrimping boats and old classic shacks. I loved the feel of Tybee Island—especially as I read a small hand-painted billboard for the Crab House that read, "Where the elite eat in their bare feet."

I pulled down a side street of Tybee and stared straight at the ocean. With goose bumps I headed to the wooden walk that led to the sand and water. I just sat for a few moments on the beach in the late afternoon. The air and colors were warm. I met a wonderful couple from Nebraska, who were visiting their son in the area, and philosophized a bit with them before I dipped my wheel into the sea.

Savannah Coastal National Wildlife Refuges protect wildlife along the Georgia coast. Just south of Tybee Island, Wassaw and Little Wassaw islands are wildlife refuges restricted to scientific observation.

LESSON: With most long journeys or goals, the end result is usually quite anti-climactic. Goals are vital—not because of what you get by achieving them, but by what you become in the process.

Afterword

I will never forget the moment in a small, sand-flea-infested gas station in Tybee Island, Georgia, when I picked up a Rand McNally Road Atlas, leafed through the first few pages to the U.S. map, and traced my finger along the 4,000-mile path I had just pedaled. As I reviewed the route, I couldn't help thinking, "What in the hell were you thinking, my man? Making these damn grandiose cross-country plans from your cozy, soft office chair in Michigan without having complete knowledge of the details involved."

Although the decision I made a year ago may not have been the most prudent, it had allowed me to find out just a little more about myself and the world around me. I was grateful that the portion of my soul that loved clear-flowing rivers had become agitated when I witnessed the sure and gradual degradation of northern Michigan's rivers. I was grateful that I'd felt a true passion and that the heavy, hollow feeling in my gut got me motivated to do something for a cause I believed in.

In this age, we are brainwashed to believe that luxury, comfort, and material wealth are the important elements in life. We scurry around to provide our families with the goods and services that slick television and radio marketing professionals make us believe we need to fulfill our lives. And during this bizarre rush, we spend less time with our families and lose sight of any sincere purpose for our lives.

Thank you for purchasing this journal, and in doing so contributing to the real stream improvement projects of the Conservation Resource Alliance. Thank you for sharing my journey with me. But do me a real favor. Step out onto your driveway, carefully lace this book with an ample volume of gasoline, and light it on fire. As you feel the heat from its flame, as you smell the nasty smoke from its pages and glue, gaze deep into the blaze and deep into your soul and find what truly moves you. Don't just read about the endeavors of others, find the courage and expend the effort to find your own unique direction. Then make a vow (not some silly, lame resolution) to follow this personal passion. This action is not about impressing your friends, it's about reconnecting your actions with your soul; it's about becoming enthusiastic in your daily living and sincerely looking yourself in the eye.

Take Action

Jeff Graft made his 4,000-mile cross-country bicycle ride because he felt it was time for him to give back something to the natural resources—and particularly the clear-flowing trout streams—that had nourished him for so many years.

We hope this book inspires you to make your own commitment to conservation, whether it is simply joining a worthy conservation group, providing some muscle and sweat to restore habitat, or making your own journey on behalf of the environment.

Here are a few important organizations that are doing much to preserve and protect bright water and ecosystems.

The Conservation Resource Alliance

The Conservation Resource Alliance (CRA) is the organization that inspired Jeff's cross-country "Ride for Rivers" to support its River Care Program, and it is the recipient of some of the profits from the sale of this book. This private, not-for-profit organization is dedicated to maintaining the rivers, streams, forests, and wildlife of northwestern Michigan. Although it is a regional organization, it has served as a model for other conservation efforts nationwide.

CRA has done wonders to bring together landowners, businesses, organizations, and governmental agencies to plan and implement the steps necessary to preserve or responsibly develop land within its

Man shapes himself through decisions that shape his environment.

Rene Dubos

thirteen-county area. One of its attractive attributes is that it serves as a single source for persons or organizations interested in working for the environment. The professionals at CRA understand the sometimes confusing and intricate regulations and funding sources. They know how to take advantage of opportunities, mobilize resources, minimize red tape, and cut through bureaucratic layers. Anyone who has ever worked on behalf of the environment knows how valuable that can be. And if you'd like to make your own contribution to the River Care Program, these are the people to contact.

Conservation Resource Alliance
Grandview Plaza Building
10850 Traverse Highway, Suite 2204
Traverse City, MI 49684
Phone: 231-946-6817
Fax: 231-947-5441

Trout Unlimited

Trout Unlimited is the nation's leading organization dedicated to the conservation, protection, and restoration of North America's trout and salmon fisheries and watersheds. It accomplishes this mission on local, state, and national levels with an extensive and dedicated volunteer network. The national office, based just outside of Washington, D.C., employs professionals who testify before Congress, publish TU's quarterly magazine, intervene in federal legal proceedings, and work with TU's 100,000 grassroots volunteers in 450 chapters nationwide to keep them active and involved in conservation issues.

Trout Unlimited
1500 Wilson Boulevard
Suite 310
Arlington, VA 22209-2404
Phone: 703-522-0200

Fax: 703-284-9400
To Join: 800-834-2419
Website: www.tu.org

American Rivers

American Rivers is a national conservation organization dedicated to protecting and restoring America's river systems and to fostering a river stewardship ethic. The organization was founded in 1973 to expand the number of rivers protected by the National Wild and Scenic Rivers System. Along with its conservation efforts, American Rivers promotes public awareness about the importance of healthy rivers and the threats to them.

American Rivers has built a strong record of enhancing grassroots river conservation efforts through its nationally recognized conservation expertise and public education. Its successes include the preservation of more than 22,000 miles of nationally and regionally significant rivers and over 5.5 million acres of riverside lands. In addition to protecting nationally significant rivers, American Rivers' programs address flood control and hydropower policy reform, endangered aquatic and riparian species protection, western instream flow, clean water, and urban rivers.

Its staff works cooperatively with conservation groups, local citizens and businesses, and various federal, state, and tribal agencies to build coalitions and provide technical support to strengthen local and regional conservation efforts which protect rivers. Based in Washington, D.C., American Rivers operates regional offices in Phoenix, Arizona and Seattle, Washington.

American Rivers, Inc. is a national, nonprofit river conservation organization recognized under IRS Tax Code 501(c)(3). They have a growing membership of 18,700 people. Its annual publications include a quarterly newsletter, annual report, and an in-depth report on North America's Most Endangered and Threatened Rivers. American Rivers receives funding through contributions from its members, corporations, and private foundations.

American Rivers
1025 Vermont Avenue, NW, Suite 720
Washington, D.C. 20005
Phone: 202-347-7550
Fax: 202-347-9240
Website: www.amrivers.org

Nature Conservancy

The mission of The Nature Conservancy is to preserve plants, animals, and natural communities that represent the diversity of life on Earth by protecting the lands and waters they need to survive.

Founded in 1951, The Nature Conservancy is the world's leading private, international conservation group. It preserves habitats and species by saving the lands and waters they need to survive.

Its one-million-plus members have helped protect more than eleven million acres of habitat in the United States and nearly sixty million acres in Canada, Latin America, the Caribbean, Asia, and the Pacific. It currently manages 1,340 preserves, the largest system of private nature sanctuaries in the world.

The Nature Conservancy's nonconfrontational approach allows them to forge partnerships with landowners, corporations, and governments. And its commitment to working with local people gives it an on-the-ground presence in communities around the world.

The Nature Conservancy
4245 North Fairfax Drive, Suite 100
Arlington, VA 22203-1606
Phone: 800-628-6860
Website: www.tnc.org